EASY
Needle
Felting

EASY
Needle
Felting

Nancy Hoerner, Judy Jacobs & Kay Kaduce

STERLING

New York / London
www.sterlingpublishing.com

Prolific Impressions Production Staff:
Editor in Chief: Mickey Baskett
Copy Editor: Phyllis Mueller
Graphics: Dianne Miller, Karen Turpin
Styling: Lenos Key
Photography: Jerry Mucklow, Joel Tressler
Indexing: Miche Baskett
Administration: Jim Baskett

Library of Congress Cataloging-in-Publication Data

Hoerner, Nancy.
 Easy needle felting / Nancy Hoerner, Judy Jacobs & Kay Kaduce.
   p. cm.
 Includes index.
 ISBN-13: 978-1-4027-4431-0
 ISBN-10: 1-4027-4431-5
1. Felting. 2. Felt work. I. Jacobs, Judy. II. Kaduce, Kay. III. Title.

TT849.5.H74 2008
746'.0463--dc22

                                                                          2007015352

2 4 6 8 10 9 7 5 3 1

Published by Sterling Publishing Co., Inc.
387 Park Avenue South, New York, NY 10016
©2007 by Prolific Impressions, Inc.
Distributed in Canada by Sterling Publishing
c/o Canadian Manda Group, 165 Dufferin Street,
Toronto, Ontario, Canada M6K 3H6
Distributed in the United Kingdom by GMC Distribution Services,
Castle Place, 166 High Street, Lewes, East Sussex, England BN7 1XU
Distributed in Australia by Capricorn Link (Australia) Pty. Ltd.
P.O. Box 704, Windsor, NSW 2756, Australia

Printed in China
All rights reserved

ISBN-13: 978-1-4027-4431-0
ISBN-10: 1-4027-4431-5

For information about custom editions, special sales, premium and corporate purchases, please contact Sterling Special Sales Department at 800-805-5489 or specialsales@sterlingpub.com.

Acknowledgements

We thank Kathy Meier for her help and inspiration.

We also thank these suppliers:

Colonial Needle and Chris Hanner (www.myfavoritethimble.com) for wool roving and pencil roving, felting needles, foam blocks, and embroidery and beading needles.

National Nonwovens, for short-fibered wool roving.

Misty Meadow (www.mistymeadowicelandics.com), for wool roving.

Double Takes Design Duo (www.doubletakedesignduo.com), for unusual wool clouds and for felting needles.

Delta, Plaid Enterprises, Inc., and American Traditional, for stencils.

Walnut Hollow Farms, Inc., for the stencil-burning tool.

X-acto, for the retractable blade knife.

Beacon Adhesives, for fabric adhesive.

Rona Horn, for lampwork beads, www.ronahorn.com

Meet the Artists

Nancy Hoerner

Nancy Hoerner is an accomplished artist and designer who has been developing her artwork over the past 30 years. Her art dolls and bead projects have been published in national magazines and are held in private collections. Nancy has studied doll making and beading with renowned artists, and she works with manufacturers in the craft industry.

Judy Jacobs

Through art classes at all levels, Judy Jacobs developed an eye for color and visual balance. For years, she has been teaching classes in fiber arts, encouraging her students to try new ideas, explore, and love art. She finds lessons from one class easily translate to other disciplines and mediums. Her employer at a yarn shop encouraged her to take a needle felting class so she could be helpful to interested customers. The resulting tote bag was the start of a satisfying, exciting adventure.

Kay Kaduce

Kay Kaduce learned to sew at age 16. She's had both a custom sewing business and a floral shop. Five years ago she began a series of books, *All Through the Home,* about do-it-yourself home decor. Now with eight books and counting, she has developed a following at home shows where she conducts workshops. Three years ago Kay began working with fiber, creating needle felted designs. She also designs patterns, teaches workshops, and is a contributor to needle felting books.

Contents

Introduction 8

Felting Glossary 9

chapter 1

Needle Felting Supplies 10

    Safety Tips 13

chapter 2

Making Felt Fabric 14

    Ruffled Clutch Purse 19

    Bold Traveler with Beaded Flap 23

    Retro Sophisticate Purse 26

    Gussied Up Tote 30

    Modern Art Clutch 32

    Josie's Cape 34

40

69

chapter 3

Needle Felted Hats 38

chapter 4

Felting a Design with Stencils 42

    Cutting a Stencil 43

    Felting the Design 44

    Warm & Comfy Fleece Throw 46

    Winter's Here Snowflake Sweater 48

    Felted Flower Tote 52

    Vine & Flower Jeans 54

    Fancy Flowered Denim Skirt 56

    Dragonfly Dimension Pillow 58

chapter 5

Free Form Felting 60

    Black Jacket with Felted Yoke 62

    Heathered Fleece Jacket 64

    Hills & Valleys Denim Jacket 66

    Colorful Strands Cardigan 68

    Cape of Cloud Jacket 72

    Pretty Petals Jacket 76

    Trimmed in Style Sweater 80

    Counting Sheep Blanket Throw 82

chapter 6

Making Felt Jewelry 86

    Making Tube Beads 87

    Making Round Beads 88

    Winter Wardrobe Necklace 89

    Amulet Bag 90

    Multi-Strand Necklace 91

    Diamond Felted Bracelet 92

    Fashion Circles Pendant Necklace 93

    Memory Wire Bracelets 94

    Beaded Fantasy Bracelet 96

    Tropical Bird Pin 98

    Embellished Bead Necklaces 99

chapter 7

Making Felted Embellishments 102

    Flowers & Leaves 104

    Fall Fantasy Flower 106

    Making Faces 108

    Silk & Sparkle Embellished Hat 112

Appendix 114

Needle Felting Gallery 118

Metric Conversion Chart 126

Index 127

A Brief History of Felting

Manipulating fiber into functional fabric is a practice that dates back centuries, and felting is thought to predate spinning, weaving, or knitting. According to some reports, felting dates as far back as 6300 BCE. Our ancestors used wool and other animal fibers, which have the unique ability to mat together, to create felt, a non-woven fabric. From felt, they made blankets, rugs, clothing, hats, boots, and even structures such as yurts.

All felting relies on the principle that wool fibers have scales – the process of felting causes these scales to mesh with neighboring fibers and lock together. The traditional process of **wet felting** involves wool, soap, water, and gentle agitation. (It's the same process that causes a wool sweater to shrink if you wash it in a washing machine.) For the hand process of felting, thin layers of carded wool are stacked, with the fibers in alternating directions. Hot water and soap are added, and the fibers are manipulated. The more manipulation, the tighter the resultant fabric becomes. The fabric can be cut with no worry of fraying.

Machine felting is an adaptation of the wet felting process that uses large machines with thousands of needles to punch the fibers. The needles have small downward barbs that interlock the wool fibers without soap and water, causing the scales of the fibers to become tangled with each other. This is how industrial felt is made.

Needle felting or **dry felting** began in the 1980s, when artisans David and Eleanor Stanwood used a tool from the woolen mill industry on a much smaller scale to create needle felted sculptured shapes by hand. The same process, using one or more felting needles, also can be used to make flat fabric. Needle felting is very simple to learn and has gained popularity over the years among artists and crafters, including quilters, dollmakers, and bear artists. It requires minimal supplies, can be done almost anywhere, and – with a bit of practice – yields beautiful, professional results.

You can make needle felted fabric, shaped items like hats or bags, or use needle felting techniques to decorate and embellish a wide variety of surfaces, including other types of fabric. Craft felt is an easy fabric to learn on. We've had great success with off-the-shelf terrycloth towels, t-shirts, wool vests, stiff fusible interfacing, hand-woven fabrics, ready-made items such as purses, all kinds of clothing, knitted/crocheted items – the possibilities are nearly endless.

This book shows you how to make a variety of needle felted items, including purses, hats, and jewelry and how to use needle felting techniques to embellish clothing and home accessories.

Felting Glossary

Carding – Aligning wool fibers by combing. Can be done by hand or on a machine.

Cloud – Wool bath with unaligned fibers. Also called **spinner's cloud**.

Craft felt – Machine-made felt (the type of felt you can buy in a craft store).

Foam block – Surface for felting made of polypropylene or polyethylene.

Foam pad – Surface for felting made of upholstery foam.

Multi-needle felting tool – A wooden holder that can hold up to 12 needles.

Needling – Punching, stabbing, or poking a felting needle into wool. *Note: "Needle" is also used as a verb to describe this technique.*

Roving – Wool that has been carded but not spun. Fibers are aligned. A **pencil roving** is a piece of wool roving that is the size of a pencil.

chapter 1

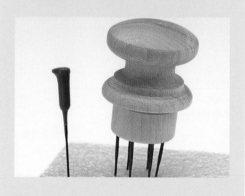

Needle Felting Supplies

Needle felting requires just a few tools: wool, a piece of foam to work on, and – of course – needles. You can find supplies at fabric, crafts, and yarn stores and online.

Felting Needles

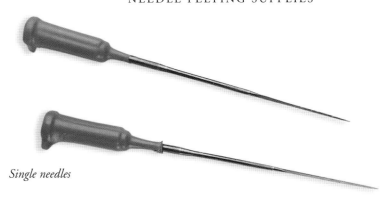

Single needles

To create felted designs, you need felting needles. There are different sizes and gauges of needles available (36, 38, and 40 are common gauges); the smaller the gauge, the larger the hole the needle makes. Some needles have varied-depth barbs. Felting needles and multiple needle tools can be found at yarn or fiber shops that sell fibers to spin and weave. You can also find them online.

Single needles are perfect for most small items and sculptural work. Some needles have the blunt end covered with a blue tip that protects your fingers and makes it easy to identify which end is the sharp one. They usually come two to a package.

Multi-needle tools have a wooden handle in which six or 12 needles can be inserted. Use these tools to create felted fabric or work in large areas of a design. The advantage of multi-needle tools is speed. A single needle can do all needle felting tasks but will take longer.

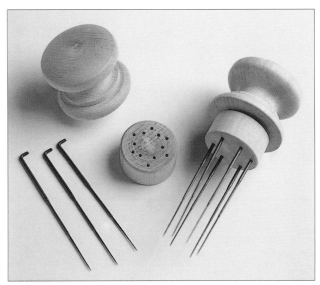

Multi-needle tools

Foam Work Surface

Working on a piece of foam allows the needle to do its punching but protects your lap or work table from the needle's point. The foam should be at least two inches thick (thicker is generally better). Polyethylene foam (the kind used to protect electronics) can be obtained at some packing supplies stores. You can also use the dense green foam (polypropylene) found in sewing centers. Upholstery foam is soft and will bounce when you work on it, but it can be cut to any size you want. Less expensive cushion foam may not be dense enough – it has too much "give" and is difficult to work with. Rigid plastic foam (e.g., Styrofoam®) does not work, it crumbles.

Foam

Fibers

Un-spun wool – wool that has not yet been made into yarn – is used for needle felting in two forms, rovings and clouds.

Roving is a long, fluffy roll of wool (most is merino wool) that has been cleaned and carded so all the fibers run one direction. An intermediate step in the creation of yarn, a roving becomes yarn after spinning. Roving can be purchased by the ounce or by the skein.

Silk Roving called silks tops is also available and can be needle felted.

Clouds are wool fibers that have been cleaned and dyed. To make them, several different colors and types of fibers are fed into a machine that combines them without aligning them. Clouds are easy to use – you can readily pluck off a small amount to work into a design. You can create your own clouds for needle felting from the huge variety of commercial wool or synthetic yarns available in stores or online – just use a pet brush to un-spin the fibers. Needle felting requires 100 percent wool fiber, but yarns used for embellishing need only be very loosely spun.

SAFETY TIPS

Felting needles are sharp and capable of causing serious injury. For your protection, observe these tips and precautions.

• Keep your eyes on the needle as you work, and **always** look where you're poking. If you look away, stop poking.

• Keep the hand not holding the needle away from the needle – that way, you won't get stuck.

• Find a comfortable spot to sit, and work on foam that is thick enough – thicker than the needle is long (at least two inches).

• Always know where your needle is and where it's going. When you pause, park the needle by sticking it into your foam surface. When you stop, place the needle in its holder.

• Keep needles away from children and pets. We know of one naughty dog that chewed up a wooden-handled holder. That he did not suffer serious injury remains a mystery.

• If you accidentally break a needle (the fragments can fly so beware), pick up the sharp pieces with a piece of tape and dispose of them properly.

• Get a tetanus shot every 10 years. If you haven't had one lately and poke yourself, get one right away. Wool is not a sterile medium – you could be injecting yourself with who knows what.

• If or when you do stick a finger with a needle, **do not** put your finger in your mouth because the human mouth is full of germs. Instead, apply intense pressure to the wound while holding the finger above your heart for two to three minutes, then cover with a bandage and some over-the-counter antibiotic ointment. Signs of infection – for which you need to see a doctor – include abnormal spreading redness, abnormal soreness of the area, fever, red streaks starting up your arm, or drainage from the wound. Don't hesitate to seek medical attention. Chances of a puncture being this bad are not great, but it is better to be safe than sorry.

Care of Your Felted Piece

Needle felted items should be hand washed gently in cold water using a soap that is formulated for washing with wool. They are definitely not "tough", but can easily be gently laundered by hand as any other fine garment.

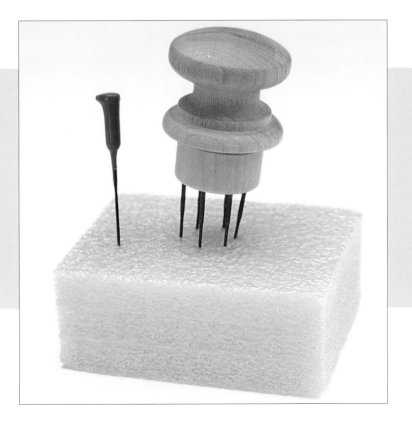

chapter 2

Making Felt Fabric

Creating your own felt fabric is a quick and satisfying process. Working with a multi-needle tool helps you create a large piece of fabric quickly. Your goal is to produce a piece of felted wool that is of an equal thickness – how thick is up to you. Hats hold up well if they are made from wool about ⅜" thick. A purse needs to be thicker to carry the weight of items you will put in it.

The wool you choose to work with determines the look and feel of your piece. Wool roving gives a wooly, homespun look. A cloud of wool mixed with synthetic fibers will produce a dressier fabric with some sparkle. Use a flat chunk of foam for making flat fabric. A foam rubber pillow bolster can be a form for a hat.

Using Fiber Clouds

1. Gather your supplies.

You need fibers in the color(s) of your choice, a foam work surface, and a multi-needle tool. Blending three or four complementary colors into one cloud brings a luxurious visual texture; combining various fibers that take dyes differently adds depth and vibrancy. Mixing colors to make the fabric means you have less control over the look of the final piece, but your fabric will be completely original.

2. Position the fibers.

Lay the wool fibers on top of the foam form in layers, alternating the direction of the fibers. (Think of a woven fabric – fibers going left and right, as well as up and down. This will produce a strong fabric when needled.) Make a stack of fibers 1½" to 2" thick.

3. Begin needling.

Start needling by punching the needle up and down into fibers, beginning at the center of the pile and working outward. Use a light poking motion with the tool.

4. Lift the fabric.

As you needle, the wool will begin to felt, forming a solid piece of fabric. When it does, lift the piece from the foam so it does not become embedded in the foam. Lift the piece often as you felt to avoid this from happening.

Using Fiber Clouds, continued

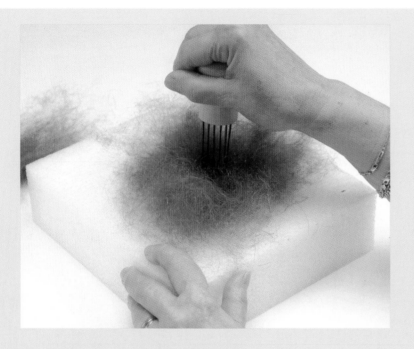

5. Continue needling both sides.

It is a good idea to turn your fabric and needle it on both sides. If you don't, the side you work on will become firm and smooth, while the other side will be fuzzier. Needling both sides makes a more consistent fabric.

When you turn the piece, hold it to the light when it is off the foam to check for thin spots. Add more fiber where the wool seems too thin and needle well. Needling for a longer time strengthens the felt fabric.

6. Making a Larger Piece

As you work, have a plan as to size, shape and thickness of the fabric. Leave loose, fuzzy edges where you want to add length, and leave a fuzzy – not firmly needled – edge if you want to join it with another piece of finished felt.

To add on or make a piece of felt longer than the piece of foam you're working on, keep the edge or edges loose and fluffy where you will be adding length. Move your first felt piece away from the center of the foam and add additional wool along the fuzzy edge.

Needle to combine the fibers. The loose, fuzzy edges will bond easily to additional fibers with little or no evidence of a seam.

Creating Finished Edges

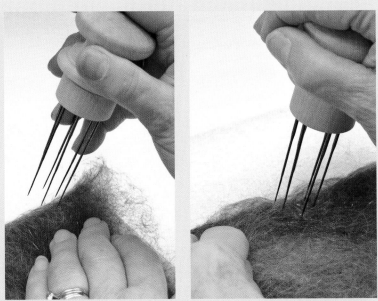

Another important concept for making needle felted fabric is knowing how to create a nicely finished edge. When you have needled a good firm piece of felt, be certain your fabric is of an overall equal thickness and is as long as the longest measurement you need. Leave the edges fuzzy.

Fold in the wispy, fuzzy edges and needle. *Option:* Use a single needle to create a straight line inside the fuzzy edge where you want your finished edge to be. When this line is needled well, brush the wispy, fuzzy ends back onto the felted fabric over the needled line. Continue needling the fuzzy ends into the fabric for a lovely invisible hem.

Finishing

Once you're happy with your needle felted fabric, finish by using a steam iron to minimize or shrink needle holes.

Hold the iron horizontally over the front side and allow the steam to penetrate.

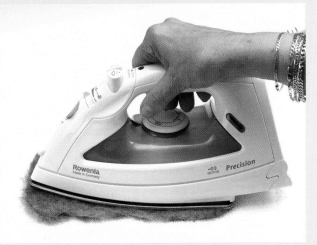

Turn over the felt and rest the iron gently on the back side. This helps flatten any tufts poking through on the back side.

Using Wool Roving

You can also make fabric using wool roving. When you have created the layers of fibers, the process for needling wool roving is the same as needling fibers from a cloud.

1. Pull apart the roving.

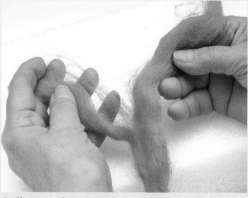

Pull apart the roving to separate the fibers — don't cut it. Pull thin pieces from the roll that are about the length of your hand.

2. Create the first layer.

Arrange short pieces of roving side by side in one direction along the foam, overlapping the pieces like shingles on a roof.

3. Continue layering.

Add pieces of roving in the opposite direction.

Continue creating layers, alternating the direction of the fibers with each layer — at least three layers are required. When the combined layers are 1½" to 2" thick, needle them to create the felt fabric.

Ruffled Clutch Purse

Instructions begin on page 20.

Ruffled Clutch Purse

You will be the envy of your lunch club. This nifty little bag is the basic clutch shape, but an added handle and a ruffle make it much more. The handles have been covered with a crocheted chain to add pizzazz.

Pictured on page 19.
Pattern on page 22.

SUPPLIES

Fibers:

- 6 oz. blue cloud or roving
- 1 skein blue and green ribbon yarn
- 1 skein bulky green wool yarn
- 1 skein blue cotton boucle yarn
- 1 skein green cotton boucle yarn
- 1 skein green fuzzy yarn

Other Supplies:

- 1 pair wooden purse handles, 6" wide
- 8 blue and green cube beads, ½"
- 27 blue and green cube beads, size 6
- Blue sewing thread
- Beading thread
- Fabric adhesive
- Magnetic snap closure

TOOLS

- Multi-needle tool and 6 felting needles, 36 gauge
- P crochet hook
- Knitting needles, size 7
- Beading needle
- Tapestry needle
- Foam pads, 12" x 18" x 3" and 2" x 2" x 8"
- Needlenose pliers
- Iron and ironing board

INSTRUCTIONS

1. Using the pattern provided, needle felt a piece of fabric for the body of the purse. See the beginning of this section for instructions on "Making Felt Fabric."
2. Fold the fabric to make the basic purse shape. (Photo 1)
3. Align the side seams and hand stitch from the top to about 2" from the bottom. (Photo 2)
4. Fold the fabric on the bottom of the purse so the bottom is flat and it forms a T-shaped seam on the side of purse. Hand stitch.
5. Place the 2" x 2" x 8" piece of foam inside the purse. (Photo 3)
6. Working one side at a time, place some wool over the T-shaped side seam. (Photo 4) Needle the wool over the side seam to cover the stitching and create a smooth look. (Photo 5) Repeat on the other side.

Crochet Handles & Trim:

1. Crochet a chain with a strand of each of the five yarns, held as one, using the P crochet hook. See "How to Crochet a Chain" in the Appendix section for instructions. *Note:* Using a P crochet hook, it takes about 1 yard of fibers to make 1 foot of trim. You will need about 2 yards of crocheted trim to cover one handle.
2. After crocheting 2 yards, but before you end the chain, wrap the trim around the handle loosely to be sure you have enough. When you do, knot the end of the chain.
3. Apply fabric adhesive to a 2" section of the handle and wrap the crocheted chain over the adhesive. (Photo 6) Continue working in 2" sections until the handle is covered with the trim.
4. Repeat steps 1 through 3 to cover the second handle.
5. Stitch the handles on the bag at the center of each side, matching the second to the first.
6. Crochet another chain about 40 inches long, using the five fibers, held as one. (The chain should be long enough to cover the top edges and sides of the purse.)
7. With a needle and thread, stitch the chain in place along the finished edges of the purse. When stitching chain onto finished edge, stitch through handles again to secure.
8. Attach the magnetic snap ½" down from the top edge at the center. Follow the package instructions and use needlenose pliers.

Add the Knitted Trim:

See "How to Knit" in the Appendix section for instructions.

1. For ruffle #1, using green wool and size 7 knitting needles, cast on 10 stitches.

   Row 1 – Knit.

   Row 2 – Knit in front and back of each stitch (20 stitches).

   Row 3 – Knit.

   Row 4 – Knit in front and back of each stitch (40 stitches).

   Row 5 – Knit.

   Row 6 – Knit in front and back of each stitch (80 stitches).

   Row 7 – Add green fuzzy yarn and bind off.

2. For ruffle #2, using the blue and green ribbon yarn, cast on 12 stitches.

   Row 1 – Knit.

   Row 2 – Knit in front and back of each stitch (24 stitches).

   Row 3 – Purl.

   Row 4 – Knit in front and back of each stitch (48 stitches).

   Row 5 – Purl.

   Row 6 – Knit in front and back of each stitch (96 stitches).

   Row 7 – Bind off.

3. Stitching with a needle and thread, sew ruffle #1 on the top edge of one side of the purse. Tack the ruffle in place about halfway down so it does not curl up.

4. Stitch ruffle #2 at the bottom edge of ruffle #1.

Finish:

Stitch assorted cube beads across the top front edge of the purse, using a beading needle and beading thread. Use the photo as a guide for placement. ❖

Photo 1 – Folding the felted fabric to make the purse shape.

Photo 2 – Hand stitching the side seams.

Photo 3 – Inserting the foam block.

Photo 4 – Placing wool over a side seam.

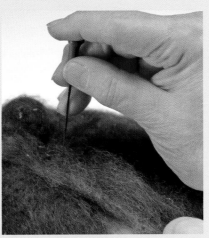

Photo 5 – Needling the wool over a side seam.

Photo 6 – Wrapping the crocheted trim around a handle.

Pattern for Ruffled Clutch Purse

Instructions on page 20.

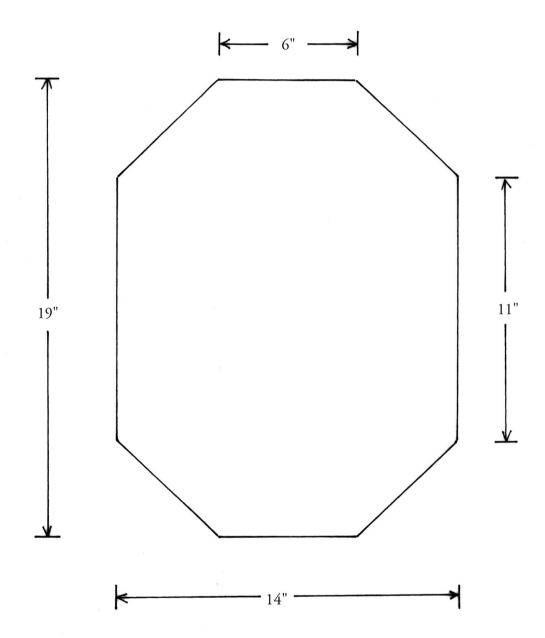

Pattern for Bold Traveler with Beaded Flap

Instructions on page 24.

Bold Traveler with Beaded Flap

This bag can be your traveling companion. Its size and shape are perfect for holding essentials. One color was used for everything on this bag - the felted fabric, the crocheted yarn trims, and the beads. We used red and like the bold statement it makes, but any single color would be effective.

Pattern appears on page 23.

SUPPLIES

Fibers:

- 7 oz. cardinal wool cloud or roving
- 1 skein red variegated ribbon yarn
- 1 skein sequin yarn
- 1 skein red and metallic mohair yarn
- 1 skein red fuzzy yarn
- 1 skein loopy yarn

Other Supplies:

- Red assorted beads, 7-1/2" strand
- 10 red seed beads, size 6
- Plastic purse handles, 6" across base
- 1/2" magnetic closure
- Red sewing thread
- Fabric adhesive

TOOLS

- Multi-needle tool and 6 felting needles, 36 gauge
- P crochet hook
- Tapestry needle
- Beading needle
- Foam pads, 18" x 24" x 3" and 2" x 2" x 8"
- Needlenose pliers
- Iron and ironing board

INSTRUCTIONS

Make the Bag:

1. Needle felt a rectangular piece of fabric from the cardinal cloud or roving for the sides of the purse. Make the rectangle 15" x 22." (The flap comes later.) See the beginning of this section for instructions on making felt fabric.
2. Fold the fabric in half to make the basic purse shape, aligning the top edges.
3. Align the side seams and hand stitch from the top to about 2" from the bottom. For guidance, see the how-to photos that accompany the "Ruffled Clutch Purse" project.
4. Fold the fabric on the bottom of the purse so the bottom is flat and it forms a T-shape on the side of purse. Hand stitch.
5. Place the 2" x 2" x 8" piece of foam inside the purse.
6. Working one side at a time, place some wool over the T-shaped side seam. Needle the wool over the side seam to cover the seam and create a smooth look. Repeat on the other side.

Make the Flap:

1. To create the flap, needle felt a piece of fabric using the pattern provided for the purse flap, finishing three sides and leaving the fourth side fluffy for attaching to the purse.
2. Attach one side of the magnetic closure according to package instructions, using needlenose pliers, at the center of the finished edge of the flap opposite the fuzzy edge. Place the clasp 1/2" to 1" from the edge. Set aside the other side of the closure.
3. Attach the fuzzy edge of the flap to the top back edge of the purse, by needling in place, working until the flap is firmly attached.

Decorate the Flap:

1. Crochet three chains, each 10" to 12" long, using the P crochet hook with various combinations of yarns. See "How to Crochet a Chain" for instructions.
2. Hand stitch the chains on the flap in a pleasing all-over design, using a tapestry needle. Use the project photo as a guide for placement.

3. Sew assorted beads to the flap in a random design, again using the photo as a guide.

Add the Handles:

1. Crochet a chain with the P crochet hook, using the five yarns as one. This will wrap around handles. One yard of yarns will make one foot of trim; two yards of crochet trim will cover one handle. Wrap the trim around the handle loosely to check the length before you knot off the crocheted chain.

2. When you have enough length, apply fabric adhesive to a 2" section of the handle and wrap the chain around the handle. Continue working in 2" sections until the handle is covered. (Working one small section at a time ensures the glue does not dry before the handle is covered.)

3. Repeat for the other handle. Let dry completely.

4. Hand stitch the handles in place, using a tapestry needle. See the photo for placement.

Finish:

1. Crochet a chain 38" long (or the circumference of the purse).

2. Using a tapestry needle and thread, stitch the chain to the top edge of the purse, also stitching it to the purse handles.

3. Install the other side of the magnetic clasp on the purse. ❖

Retro Sophisticate Purse

Marilyn Monroe probably had a bag just like this – or wished she had. When you carry this bright pink bag with its fluffy trim, you will be the envy of all your girlfriends.

SUPPLIES

Fibers:

- 6 oz. pink wool cloud
- 1 skein black cotton boucle yarn
- 1 skein black fuzzy yarn
- 1 skein black and white eyelash yarn

Other Supplies:

- 20 black and white glass beads, ½" to ¾" (with holes large enough for the #6 wire)
- 48" copper wire, #6 (Available at hardware stores.)
- Snap closure
- 30" black bangle trim
- Black sewing thread
- ¼ yd. black and white knitted fabric (for lining)

TOOLS

- Multi-needle tool and 6 felting needles
- Foam rubber bolster
- P crochet hook
- Wire cutters
- Needlenose pliers
- Tapestry needle
- Straight pins
- Fabric adhesive
- Sewing machine
- Iron and ironing board

Supplies for purse

INSTRUCTIONS

Make the Base:

1. Needle felt the purse shape on the end of the bolster, following the basic instructions for making needle felted hats. See "Needle Felted Hats" for details. The finished height of the purse sides is 7".
2. When the length is right, hem invisibly. See "Creating Finished Edges."

Install the Lining:

1. From the lining fabric, cut one piece 30" x 7" (or the circumference of your purse plus ½" for a seam allowance x 7"). Also cut a circle 9" in diameter.
2. Machine stitch the two short ends of the rectangular piece with right sides together to make a tube, using a ½" seam allowance.
3. With wrong sides together, pin the tube around the 9" circle. Machine stitch, using a ¼" seam allowance.
4. Place the lining inside the purse and pin in place around the top. (Photo 1)

Continued on page 24

Retro Sophisticate Purse, continued

5. Attach a magnetic closure to the lining, following the package directions and using needlenose pliers.
6. Hand stitch the lining in place.

Trim the Top:

1. Crochet two identical chains, each 29" long (or the circumference of the top edge of your purse), with a strand of each of the three yarns held as one, using a P crochet hook. See "How to Crochet a Chain" in the Appendix section for instructions. Set aside.
2. Hand stitch the bangle trim along the top edge of the purse.
3. Hand stitch one crocheted chain along the top edge of the purse to cover the ribbon edge of the bangle trim.
4. Hand stitch the other crocheted chain on the inside top edge to cover the edge of the lining.

Make the Handles:

1. Cut two 24" lengths of #6 copper wire.
2. Bend one piece of wire to form one side of handle and curl on end with needlenose pliers, using the pattern as a guide.
3. Thread eight beads on the wire. Bend the other end of wire as you did the first, holding the glass beads in place in the center of the handle. (Photo 2)

4. Place a small amount of fabric adhesive beside the bead on one end. Holding cotton boucle yarn and black and white eyelash yarn as one, wrap the handle with yarn to cover it completely. (Photo 3) Add adhesive about every 1" and wrap until the copper wire is completely covered. Repeat this step to finish the other side of the handle.
5. Repeat steps 2 through 4 to make the other handle.
6. Position one handle on one side of the purse. Hand stitch in place all around the curled end of wire through the crocheted trim. Hand stitch the other side of the handle.
7. Repeat step 6 to attach the other handle.

Finish:

1. Crochet three chains – one 14" long, one 12" long, and one 8" long – with a strand each of the three yarns held as one, using a P crochet hook.
2. Fasten the remaining beads on the ends of the chains. Fold the chains in half.
3. Using the photo as a guide, hand stitch in place at the top edge of the right side of the purse about 2" from the handle to form a tassel. ❖

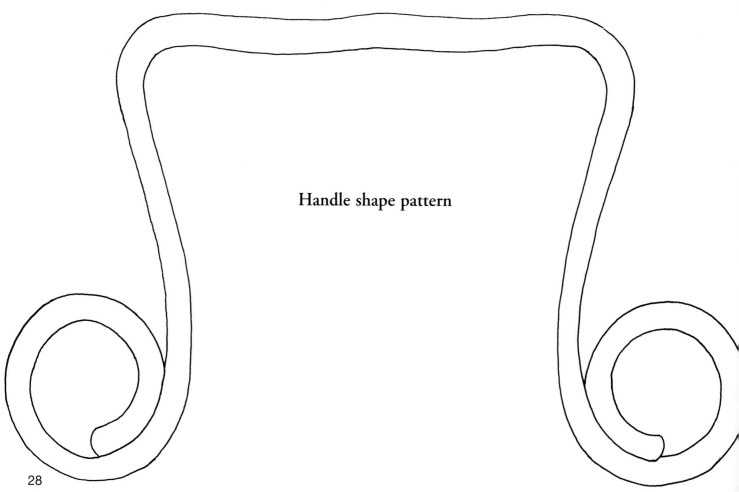

Handle shape pattern

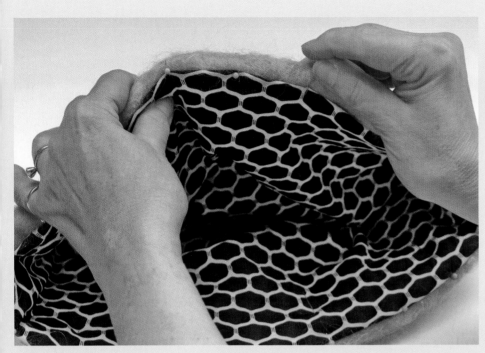

Photo 1 – Pinning the lining in place.

Photo 2 – Bending the copper wire to make a handle.

Photo 3 – Wrapping the handle with yarn.

Gussied Up Tote

This blue felted bag with a knitted gusset is the perfect size and shape for taking with you on your shopping trips. Needle felted sides and a skinny knitted scarf used for the gusset combine to make a charming tote bag. If you can knit a simple scarf, you can make this bag.

SUPPLIES

Fibers:
- 4 oz. blue wool roving
- 1 skein orange thick-and-thin wool yarn
- 1 skein multi-color lumpy yarn

Other Supplies:
- 1 pair orange plastic purse handles, 6" at the base
- Orange pearl cotton thread

TOOLS
- Multi-needle tool and 6 felting needles
- Foam pad, 12" x 12" x 3"
- P crochet hook
- Knitting needles, size 13
- Tapestry needle
- Long straight pins
- Iron and ironing board

INSTRUCTIONS

Make the Felt:
From the blue roving, needle felt two pieces of fabric, each 7" x 9". See the beginning of this section for instructions on making felt fabric.

Knit the Gusset:
See "How to Knit" in the Appendix section for instructions.
1. On size 13 knitting needles, cast on 13 stitches with both yarns held together as one.
2. Knit back and forth until this piece measures 24" long. Bind off.

Assemble:
1. With the right sides of the felt fabric facing outward, pin the knitted gusset into place along the short sides and one long side of the felt pieces to form the bag.
2. Using pearl cotton and a tapestry needle, hand sew the gusset to the felt, making a stitch about every ¼".

Finish:
1. Using both yarns and a P crochet hook, work two chains, each 9" long. See "How to Crochet a Chain" for instructions. Hand stitch to the top edge of the bag with pearl cotton.
2. Stitch the handles in place with pearl cotton on the inside of bag where the crocheted chain and felted fabric meet.
3. To make the tassel, cut three 7" lengths of lumpy yarn and tie an overhand knot in one end. Stitch to one side of one handle with pearl cotton.
4. To make the flower, cut 18" of thick and thin yarn. Wrap it around four fingers to make about 12 loops. Wrap the end of the yarn around the centers of the loops four times. Stitch through the centers with pearl cotton to hold the flower shape, then sew in place on top of the tassel. Stitch through all the layers, including the felt fabric. ❖

Modern Art Clutch

Here's a purse that will go with you to dinner. Yarn is used to make a simple swirl design on this felted bag. This quick and simple beginner's project makes a wonderful gift. Once you've made one, you'll think of numerous variations.

SUPPLIES

Fibers:

- 2 oz. wool cloud or roving
- 3 yds. thick-and-thin coordinating yarn

Other Supplies:

- 1 button (to match yarn)
- Sewing thread (to match bag)
- Magnetic closure
- *Optional:* Sewing thread to match yarn (if yarn isn't wool)

TOOLS

- Foam pad, 12" x 12" x 3"
- Multi-needle tool and felting needles
- Single felting needle
- Sewing needle
- Needlenose pliers
- Iron and ironing board

INSTRUCTIONS

Make the Felt:

1. Place four layers of wool on the foam pad, alternating directions. Needle the fibers from the center outward to form a rectangle approximately 8" x 20" and ¼" to ⅜" thick. See the beginning of this section for instructions on making felt fabric. The rectangle should be well needled; remember to release the wool from the foam often and needle both sides.
2. Finish the edges. See "Creating Finished Edges."
3. Decide which side of your piece you want as the outside and lay it face up on the foam.

Add the Trim:

Arrange the yarn trim on the felt, creating a pleasing design of loops and swirls. *If the yarn is wool,* needle it in place firmly, using a single felting needle. *If the yarn is not wool,* hand stitch it to the surface using a sewing needle and thread.

Finish:

1. Fold the rectangle into thirds to form the clutch shape, overlapping one end to form the flap.
2. Using a needle and thread, hand stitch the sides carefully, hiding the stitches as you work.
3. Apply the magnetic closure, following the package directions and using needlenose pliers.
4. Stitch the button on the flap, placing it on top of the closure to conceal it. ❖

Josie's Cape

This toasty little cape is a snap to needle felt and can be decorated to suit your dog. The pattern is sized to fit a small to medium dog, but it's easy to add width at the shoulder or length down the center back. (Chances are, your dog won't be fussy about the fit.)

Pattern appears on page 37.

SUPPLIES

Fibers:
- 2 oz. cloud or roving
- Various yarns in coordinating colors (to create the plaid)

Other Supplies:
- Thread (to match wool)
- Toggle closure

TOOLS
- Multi-needle tool and felting needles
- Single felting needle
- Foam pad, 18" x 24" x 3"
- Straight pins
- Large-eye tapestry needle
- Sewing needle
- Iron and ironing board

INSTRUCTIONS

Make the Felt Base:

See the beginning of this section for instructions on making felt fabric.

1. Trace the pattern, enlarge as needed, and cut out the shape.
2. Place wool roving over the foam pad with layers of fibers in opposite directions to make a sturdy fabric.
3. Place the pattern on the roving. Use straight pins to outline the pattern shape. (Photo 1) Remove the pattern.
4. Needle the wool inside the pins to make the felt fabric, working from the center outward. (Photo 2) As the wool begins to felt, release it from the foam. Check for weak spots and fill them in with extra wool. Replace pattern and pins after releasing. Turn the felt and needle both sides. The entire piece should be about ⅜" thick.
5. Needle the wool about ½" beyond the pins. (Photo 3) Remove the pins, turn the hem, and needle to secure. See "Creating Finished Edges."

continued on next page

Photo 1 – Outlining the pattern shape with pins.

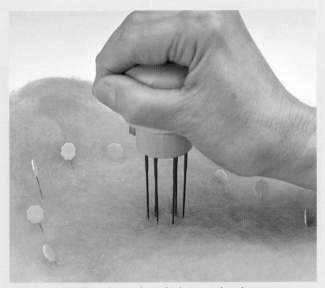

Photo 2 – Needling the wool inside the pinned outline.

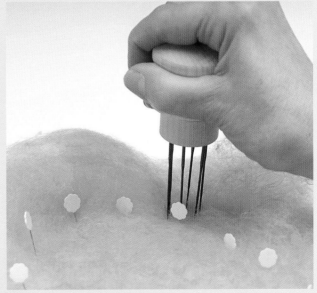

Photo 3 – Needling the wool outside the pinned outline.

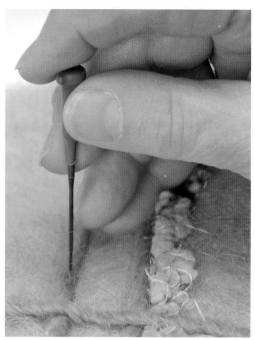

Photo 4 – Using a single needle to attach the wool yarn to form the plaid.

Josie's Cape, continued

Create the Plaid:

1. Using the photo as a guide, lay the yarns on the surface of the felt. TIP: Work one color at a time so the pattern of the plaid will be consistent.

2. *If you're using wool yarns, needle them in place using a single felting needle. (Photo 4) As you work, leave 1½" to 2" tails at the edge.* If the yarns you're using aren't made of wool, attach them using a sewing needle and thread. As you work, leave 1½" to 2" tails at the edge.

3. When all the yarns are attached to the surface, use the large-eye tapestry needle to draw the tails into the wool like this: Push the point of the needle into the center of the fabric, thread the yarn tail, and draw it inside to secure. This leaves the edges clean and crisp. (Photo 5)

Add the Closure:

1. Cut a buttonhole large enough to accept the toggle. Stitch around the edges of the buttonhole to reinforce it.

2. Attach the toggle using a needle and thread. ❖

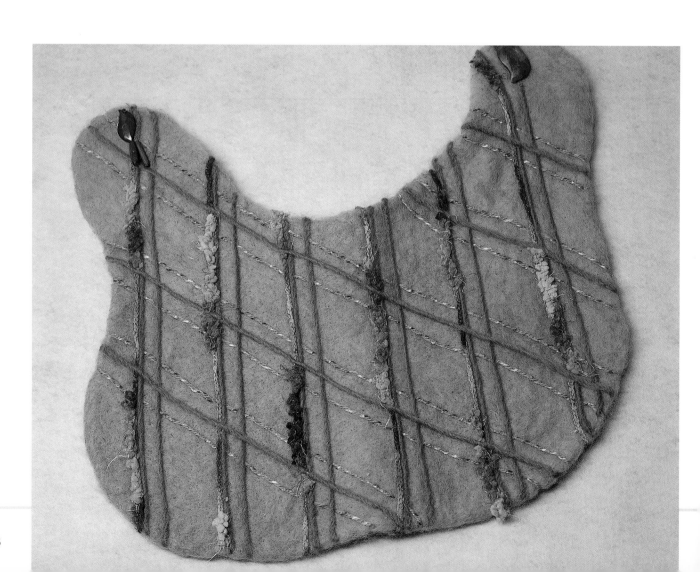

Pattern for Josie's Cape

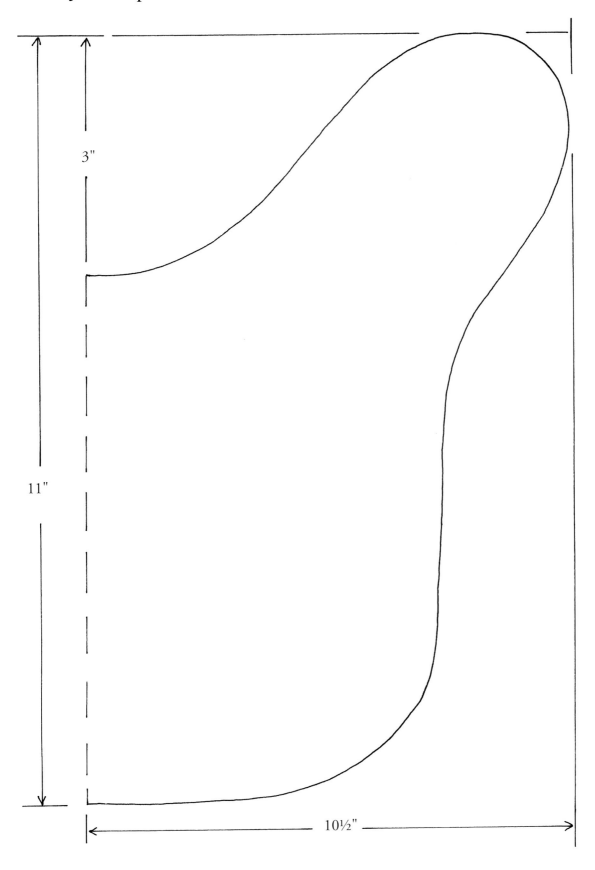

3"

11"

10½"

chapter 3

Needle Felted Hats

A needle felted hat is made in much the same way as needle felted fabric, except that the hat is made on a foam bolster or other rounded shape so it will fit the shape of the head. The same dimensional technique can be used to make other shaped items, such as purses.

Many of us love hats and feel wonderful in them, while others believe they don't look good in hats. How you look in a hat depends on the shape of your face and the shape of the hat. Some faces look great framed equally on each side by the hat brim, while others need a hat brim that is longer on one side. The basic hat offered here can be made to work for either circumstance. When you turn the brim, you can make the same width all around or you can gently pull one side to elongate the shape.

You can decorate the turned brim with a favorite brooch, yarn bands, or needle felted flowers. (See "Making Flowers & Leaves" for instructions.) Enjoy!

SUPPLIES

Fibers:

- 4 oz. cloud *or* 4 oz. roving
- 2½ oz. cloud *or* roving (for trim)
- DK yarn (double knit or sport weight)

TOOLS

- Multi-needle tool and felting needles
- Single felting needle
- Cylindrical foam bolster, 6" x 12" (Measure the circumference and compare with your head measurement – you may need a different size.)

INSTRUCTIONS

Make the Top of the Crown:

1. Place the bolster between your knees or on a table with one end facing you. To make the top of the crown, place three or four layers of wool fibers on the end of the bolster, alternating the direction of the fibers. (Think of a woven fabric – fibers going left and right, as well as up and down. This will produce a strong fabric when needled.) Make a stack of fibers 1½" to 2" thick.

2. Begin needling in the center of the stack of fibers, working outward and using light poking strokes. As the wool begins to felt, turn it over occasionally to prevent it from becoming stuck to the foam form. This is very important! Leave the edges fluffy and loose so you can add more wool seamlessly.

Make the Sides:

1. When the top of the crown is nicely felted and you cannot see light through it easily, begin adding wool to the sides of the bolster to make the sides of the crown and the brim of the hat. Remember to place the fibers lengthwise (up and down) as well as around the cylinder. This creates a strong fabric.

Photo 1 – Needling the sides of the hat.

Photo 2 – Adding wool to extend the sides of the hat.

Photo 3 – Using a single needle to mark the bottom edge.

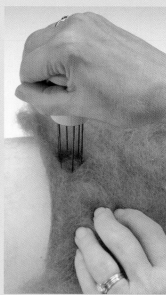

Photo 4 – Forming the bottom edge.

2. Needle the wool. (Photo 1) Continue releasing and turning the hat as you work. Be very gentle as you loosen and turn the felted shape – if you stretch it, it will be difficult to make it smaller again. Needle both sides of the fabric well and check for light through the fibers as you turn it – light indicates weak spots; add wool and needle. Continue adding wool and needling (Photo 2) to the sides until they are 6½" to 7" long.

3. When the length is right, use the single needle to create a straight line inside the fuzzy edge. (Photo 3) This line will be the bottom edge.

4. When the line is well-needled, brush the wispy, fuzzy ends back toward the hat shape over the needled line and use the multi-needle tool to form the bottom edge of the hat, which will be the hat brim. (Photo 4)

5. Remove the hat from the form and try it on. Turn up the brim as desired, shaping it gently with your hands.

Hat Variation with Knitted Band & Ruffle Flower

Pictured opposite.

This gray hat is a cloche style. It was formed according to the basic instructions, but when the sides of the hat were 6½" to 7" long, an additional 2" was added to one side. The longer side was shaped to join the shorter side and hemmed.

This hat was trimmed with a 2" wide band of knitted novelty yarn. The flower was knitted with DK weight yarn, using a pair of #8 single-point knitting needles. The finished flower was stitched to the hat.

Knitting Instructions for Ruffle Flower

Knitting the stitches together makes one edge much longer than the other; the piece will ruffle. See "How to Knit" in the Appendix section for instructions.

1. Using DK yarn, cast on 120 stitches and knit 1 row.
2. Row 2 – Knit 2 stitches together across the row.
3. Row 3 – Knit across 60 stitches.
4. Row 4 – Bind off as you knit two stitches together.
5. Wrap the ruffle on itself to form a rose. Hand stitch to secure with a needle and thread.

chapter 4

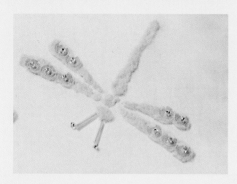

Felting a Design with Stencils

Add a needle felted design on an article of clothing or home décor item is an easy and rewarding way to put a motif on fabric. Using a stencil for the design makes it that much easier. For best results, select a stencil design with a simple, separated motif or a stencil with just one large opening.

You can buy pre-cut stencils or cut your own using stencil blank material. Don't use metal stencils for needle felting – they can break the needles.

The fabric items you decorate with needle felting need not be 100 percent wool or even a wooly synthetic, but the fabric base does need to be sturdy enough that the stabbing of the needle does not degrade it. Also, it should be of a fabric that will not shrink and change the character of the design. We've used fleece, denim, and canvas in addition to a wool sweater. The techniques are the same. We don't recommend fabrics that might snag (such as silk or satin) and we don't use suede or vinyl; punching them with the needle weakens them.

Cutting a Stencil

Stencil Cutting Supplies

- A pattern
- Stencil blank material
- A fine-tip marker
- A craft knife and self-healing cutting mat *or* an electric stencil burner and a ceramic tile
- A face mask (if you're using an electric burner)

1. Trace the design.

Place the pattern on your work surface. Place the stencil blank material over the pattern. Trace the design on the stencil material, using a marker. Remove the pattern.

2. Cut design with a craft knife.

Place the stencil blank material on the self-healing mat and cut out the design, using a craft knife with a sharp blade.

3. Cut design with an electric burner (optional).

Heat the stencil burner. Position the stencil blank material on the ceramic tile. Go over the traced design with the heated stencil point of the burner. Wear a face mask and work in a well-ventilated area to protect yourself from fumes.

Felting the Design

1. Position the stencil.

Start by positioning the stencil on the fabric article you wish to decorate. Use masking tape to hold the stencil in place.

2. Place on a foam block.

Place the area to be decorated, with the stencil attached, on a foam block.

3. Place wool in the stencil openings.

Place small tufts of short-fibered wool cloud or roving inside the stencil openings. For best results, use small amounts of wool, needle it, then add more.

4. Needle the wool.

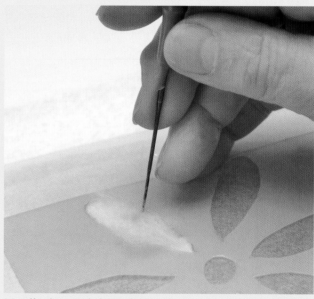

Needle the wool through the stencil openings into the background fabric, using a single felting needle.

5. Clean up the edges.

Move your finger across the stencil, turn loose wisps of wool toward the stencil opening, and needle down the stray fibers. Repeat steps 3, 4, and 5 to complete all parts of the stencil.

6. Remove the stencil.

Remove the stencil carefully, lifting it off the felted design.

7. Clean up the edges again.

Use a single needle to clean up any remaining wisps of wool, turning them into the stencil design and needling them until they are flat.

8. Finish.

Hold a steam iron above the felted area on both sides to remove needle marks and secure the fibers. Press with the iron to flatten the felted design.

The back side of the stencil-decorated design.

Warm & Comfy Fleece Throw

Felted daisies decorate this plain fleece throw, making it very enticing. What a great way to personalize or add some pizzazz to a plain inexpensive throw. Similar throws can be purchased at most shops that sell bed linens. You can buy daisy stencils or cut your own using the pattern provided and instructions at the beginning of this section. If you buy stencils, look for ones with sticky backs – they are easy to use on fabric.

SUPPLIES
- Fleece throw
- Daisy stencil
- Short-fibered wool cloud or roving – White, yellow gold

TOOLS
- Felting needle
- Foam block
- Masking tape (for holding the stencils in place, unless you're using the sticky kind)
- Iron and ironing board

INSTRUCTIONS
See the basic instructions at the beginning of this section. If you are cutting your own stencil, use a copier to enlarge or reduce the daisy pattern to whatever size you wish.

1. Place the throw on a hard, flat surface. Position the stencils on one corner of the throw. *If you're using sticky stencils,* press down on the stencils, running your finger around each open section to secure them in place. *If you've cut your own stencils,* secure them in place with masking tape.
2. Using small amounts of wool, needle the design through the stencil openings. Keep adding wool until the designs are solid but not heavy and wisps do not extend beyond the stencil openings. Use white wool for the petals and yellow gold for the flower centers.
3. Remove the stencil. Clean up around the centers and each petal, needling until the wool is almost flat on the fabric surface.
4. Add as many daisies to throw as you wish.
5. Press the front and back of the felted designs with a steam iron. ❖

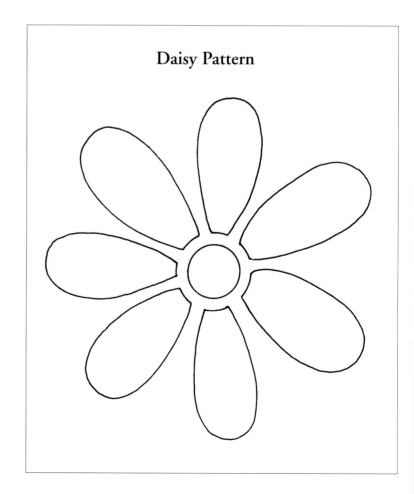

Daisy Pattern

"Winter's Here" Snowflake Sweater

Let those cold winds blow! This snowflake sweater will keep you cozy. Any plain jacket or sweater can be decorated quickly with this technique. We've provided patterns for cutting your own snowflake stencils; you could also buy pre-cut ones. Because no two snowflakes are alike, some snowflakes were created using parts of two or three stencils. If you are cutting your own stencil, use a copier to enlarge or reduce the daisy pattern to whatever size you wish.

SUPPLIES

- Red sweater
- 1-2 oz. white short-fibered wool roving *or* cloud

TOOLS

- Foam block, 12" x 12" x 3"
- Snowflake stencils
- Single felting needles
- Safety pins
- Masking tape
- Iron and ironing board

INSTRUCTIONS

1. To determine the placement of the snowflakes, try on the sweater. Select the sites by looking in a mirror or having a friend help. Put a safety pin where you want to place each snowflake. Place larger flakes near the bottom, and place medium and smaller flakes on the top. Take off the sweater.
2. Place the area of the sweater you want to stencil first on top of the foam pad, right side up. Position the stencil on the sweater and secure with masking tape.
3. Place and needle small bits of wool in the open spaces. Work with the needle straight up and down; if the needle is at a slant you could distort the stencil design.
4. When the area inside the stencil is filled, remove the stencil and touch up any fuzzy edges to clarify the snowflake design.
5. Repeat steps 2 and 3 until each snowflake is finished and well needled.
6. Working on the inside of the sweater with the iron as hot as the fiber content of the sweater will allow, press carefully to heat set the wool. ❖

Snowflake Patterns

Enlarge to size of your choice.

Pattern for Felted Flower Tote

Instructions begin on page 52.

Felted Flower Tote

Seems like we always have something to tote around.
Canvas totes are quite handy for this *and* inexpensive – but
so plain. Now you can jazz up your plain totes with the easy
needle felting technique. Use any design you like to
personalize your tote.

SUPPLIES

- Natural canvas tote bag, 13½" square
- Short-fibered wool roving or cloud –
  Olive green, rust, gold
- Brown seed beads
- White beading thread

TOOLS

- Single felting needle
- Multi-needle tool and felting needles
- Foam block
- Beading needle
- Stencil cutting supplies *or* flower stencil
- Template material
- Masking tape
- Iron and ironing board
- Fabric adhesive

Pattern appears on page 51.

INSTRUCTIONS

1. Using the pattern provided, cut the flower stencil. See "Cutting a Stencil."
2. Position the stencil on the canvas bag and secure with masking tape.
3. Slip the foam block into the bag under the stencil.
4. Needle felt the design, using the gold wool for the flower center, rust wool for the flower petals and bud, and olive green wool for the stems and leaves.
5. When the needling is finished, remove the stencil and clean up the edges of the design.
6. Press both the front and back of the felted area with a steam iron.
7. Using a beading needle and beading thread, sew three-bead clusters around the design, using the photo as a guide for placement. Sew beads on the flower center for a textured look.
8. Make a piece of rust-colored flat felted fabric large enough from which to cut out five petals. See "Making Felt Fabric" for instructions.
9. Trace one petal of the flower stencil on a piece of template material to use as a pattern. Cut out five petals from the felted fabric.
10. Use fabric adhesive to attach the cutout petals to the felted flower on the tote bag, covering the spaces between the petals. ❖

Vine & Flower Jeans

We used two border stencils to create the vine-and-flower design on these jeans. When stenciling on garments, avoid working on areas with seams. Here, the side seam of the jeans leg was used to align the stencil designs. Hand wash and dry your jeans that have been decorated with needle felting.

SUPPLIES

- Denim jeans
- Short-fibered wool roving or cloud – Magenta, red, orange, light green, dark green
- Red seed beads
- Pearl seed beads
- Pink flower sequins, ½"
- Beading thread – White, red

TOOLS

- Vine-and-leaf stencil, 8½" long
- Flower stencil with 1½" flowers, 8½" long
- Masking tape
- Felting needle
- Foam block
- Beading needle
- Iron and ironing board

INSTRUCTIONS

1. Position vine and leaf stencil along the side seam of one leg on the jeans and secure with masking tape.
2. Place the foam block inside the jeans leg. With small amounts of wool – dark green for the vines and light green for the leaves – needle through the holes in the stencil. Keep adding wool until the motif is solid, but not heavy, and is not sticking out of the stencil. Reposition the foam block as needed as you work.
3. Remove the stencil and reposition to add a vine with a curl at the end. Needle felt the vine and curl with dark green wool roving. Remove the stencil and clean up around the edges of the motifs.
4. Position the flower stencil and secure with masking tape. Working one flower at a time, make the flowers. All the flower centers are yellow; the flower petals are magenta, red, and orange. Remove the stencil and clean up around the edges of the motifs.
5. Go over the entire design, needling to felt the wool flat to the denim. Remove the foam block.
6. Press the front and back of the felted design with a steam iron. (This flattens the felting and removes the needling holes.)
7. Using red beading thread, sew clusters of three red seed beads, placing the beads about ¼" apart. Place as many clusters throughout the design as you wish.
8. Using white thread, sew the flower-shaped sequins and pearls to the jeans, scattering them throughout the design. Bring the thread up from the wrong side, put on one sequin and one pearl bead, go back through the sequin, and knot off. ❖

Fancy Flowered Denim Skirt

Felting and beads provide colorful accents on a simple denim skirt. Hand wash and dry your garments that have been decorated with needle felting.

SUPPLIES

- Denim skirt
- Short-fibered wool roving – Yellow, pale blue, rose, lavender, light green, dark green
- Seed beads – Yellow, pearl
- Pearl flower-shaped sequins, ⅛" diameter
- Beading thread – Yellow, white

TOOLS

- Stencil with vine, leaves, and flowers, 8½" long
- Beading needle
- Masking tape
- Felting needle
- Foam block
- Iron and ironing board

INSTRUCTIONS

1. Position the stencil along the side seam of the skirt and secure with masking tape. Position the foam block under the stencil.
2. Using small amounts of wool, needle through the holes in the stencil. Use yellow wool for the flower centers, light green for leaves, dark green for the vine, and pale blue, rose, and lavender for the flower petals. Use the photos as guides for color placement. Keep adding wool until the motif is solid, but not heavy, and is not sticking out of the stencil.
3. Remove stencil and clean up around the felted motifs by needling in the loose fibers. Continue to needle until the wool designs are almost flat against the fabric surface. Remove the foam block.
4. Iron the front and back of the felted design with a steam iron. (This flattens the felting and removes the needling holes.)
5. With yellow beading thread in the beading needle, sew clusters of three yellow seed beads, spacing the beads about ¼" apart. Knot off the thread after each cluster. Place as many clusters throughout the design as you wish.
6. Sew a multi-bead cluster of yellow seed beads at the center of the rose flower.
7. Using white thread, sew flower-shaped sequins to the skirt, scattering them throughout the design. Bring the thread up from the wrong side, put on one sequin and one pearl seed bead, go back through the sequin, and knot off. ❖

Dragonfly Dimension Pillow

Subtle colors and simple felting add a new dimension to
this accent pillow. Sequins and seed beads give the
dragonfly wings their natural iridescent characteristic.

SUPPLIES

- Pillow cover, with an 8⅜" center square
- Short-fibered wool roving – Pale green
- Large iridescent sequins
- Clear seed beads
- White bugle beads
- Beading thread – White
- Pillow form to fit pillow cover

TOOLS

- Sticky-back dragonfly stencil
- Felting needle
- Foam block
- Beading needle
- Iron and ironing board

INSTRUCTIONS

1. Remove the backing from stencil and position it near the center of the pillow, using the photo as a guide for placement. Press the stencil into place and press firmly around the openings with your fingers. Place the foam block inside the pillow cover under the stencil area.

2. With small amounts of green short fibered wool, needle the design through the stencil openings.

3. Remove the stencil and clean up around the sections of the design.

4. Position the dragonfly stencils in another area, using the photo as a guide.

5. Repeat steps 2 and 3.

6. Continue to needle the motifs until wool is almost flat to the fabric surface. Remove the foam block.

7. Press the front and back of the felted design with a steam iron.

8. Using the beading thread and beading needle, sew sequins and seed beads to the dragonfly wings like this: Knot the thread, come up from the back, put a sequin and a seed bead on the thread, and go back through the sequin to the back of the fabric. Sew three sequins on the top wings and two on the bottom wings of each dragonfly.

9. Sew a pair of bugle beads with a seed bead at the end of each one to make the antennae of each dragonfly. ❖

chapter 5

Free Form Felting

It's not necessary to create wool fabric or use design motifs such as stencils to enjoy a garment that is a beautiful example of needle felting. In this section, we feature different techniques for enhancing otherwise plain, ready-made garments. We call this free form felting.

For free form felting, wool roving or cloud is placed lightly over the base garment and firmly needled to the base, using light poking stabs with a needle tool.

Embellishments can be added to create patterns or random designs. Colors may be joyously wild, or subtle and elegant. The only limitation is your own imagination – there's no "wrong" way to do it.

Pictured right: Black Jacket with Felted Yoke. See the following page for instructions.

Black Jacket with Felted Yoke

Wool cloud or roving creates a front and back "yoke" on this simple jacket. When the wool is firmly needled in place, it's decorated with randomly placed lines of thick-and-thin wool yarn and faceted glass beads. The plain buttons on the jacket front were replaced with a variety of black glass ones. You could also do this with a cardigan sweater.

SUPPLIES

- Unlined black jacket *or* sweater
- 1 oz. wool cloud *or* roving, color(s) of your choice
- 1 skein thick-and-thin wool yarn
- 150 black faceted glass beads, ⅜"
- 5 assorted black glass buttons
- Black sewing thread

TOOLS

- Multi-needle tool and 6 felting needles, 36 gauge
- Foam pad, 12" x 12" x 3"
- Beading needle
- Iron and ironing board

INSTRUCTIONS

Create the Felted Area:

Modify the instructions to suit your jacket. Remove buttons before felting to prevent needle breakage.

1. Place the foam block inside the jacket under the area where you want to start needling. Lay the wool cloud or roving on the jacket and needle with the multi-needle tool. (Photo 1)
2. If your jacket has a collar, needle felt wool on the right side of the collar, leaving fluffy edges. Turn over the collar, turn the fluffy ends of the wool over the edge of the collar, and felt the wrong side carefully to secure the fluffy ends and cover the edges of the collar.
3. If your jacket has pockets, add wool to the tops of the pockets and needle felt, leaving fluffy edges at the tops of the pockets. Turn the wool over the top edges to the insides of the pockets and felt. Pull open the pocket gently to release the fibers and prevent the pocket from being felted closed.

Photo 1 – Using the multi-needle tool to felt the yoke area.

Photo 2 – Using a single needle to attach the yarn trim.

4. Press all the felting on the wrong side, using a steam iron set on the "wool" setting to lock down all fibers. **Note:** If your jacket or sweater contains man-made fibers, take care and use a cooler iron setting.

Add the Trim:

1. Needle felt the thick-and-thin yarn over the felted wool in a meandering pattern, using a single needle. (Photo 2) You can make your own design or use the photo as a guide.

2. Stitch black beads over the yarn, placing them individually or in clusters every 1" to 1½". Use a beading needle and beading thread. Use the photo as a guide for placement.

3. If you are replacing the buttons from the jacket, sew the assorted black glass buttons on in their places. ❖

Pictured below: Jacket Pocket

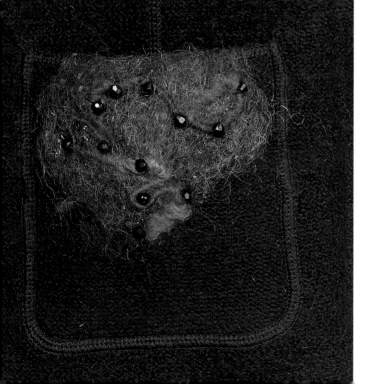

Heathered Fleece Jacket

Wool in colors of heather is added around the back neckline and front shoulder area. It's a beautiful way to add an "artsy" statement to any jacket or sweater.

SUPPLIES

- Fleece jacket
- Green wool cloud mixture (mix contains green, purple, plus metallic threads)
- Beads, various sizes and shapes – Pink, green
- Green beading thread

TOOLS

- Single felting needle
- Multi-needle tool and felting needles
- Foam block
- Beading needle
- Iron and ironing board

INSTRUCTIONS

1. Divide the cloud in half and open it out, then drape it across one shoulder of the jacket around the neck edge, using the photo as a guide. Create open spaces by pulling the cloud. Keep the outer edge of the cloud irregular.
2. Place the part of the jacket to be felted over the foam block.
3. Using the single felting needle, secure the cloud here and there.
4. Using the multi-needle felting tool, needle the cloud to the jacket. Continue until the piece is felted firmly.
5. Iron the back and front of the felted area with a steam iron.
6. Using the beading needle and beading thread, sew clusters of beads in some of the open areas and in some of the felted areas, again using the photo as a guide. ❖

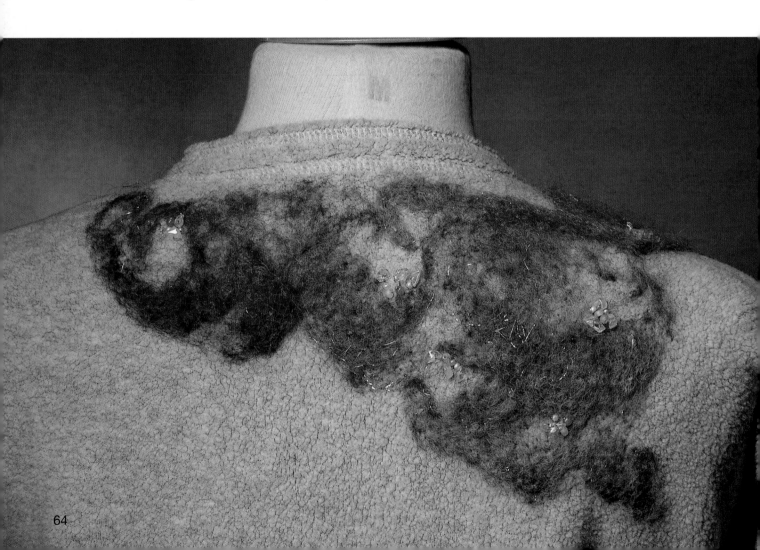

Hills & Valleys Denim Jacket

If denim is your "uniform," here is a way to make it a little more free-form and fun. Strands of wool roving are laid on the yoke areas of a denim jacket to create a fantasy landscape. Lines of beads accent the design.

SUPPLIES

• Denim jacket

• Wool roving – Teal, turquoise, lime green

• Silver-lined turquoise triangle beads

• Round silver-lined turquoise beads, 8mm

• Oval silver beads, 3mm x 4mm

• Round silver beads, 4mm

• Blue beading thread, size B

TOOLS

• Single felting needle

• Multi-needle tool and felting needles

• Beading needle

• Foam block

• Iron and ironing board

INSTRUCTIONS

1. Pull the teal roving into long strands and lay it in a hill and valley pattern along the back yoke, right front yoke, front buttonhole panel of the jacket. Needle felt in place over the foam block.

2. Following the same design lines, lay turquoise and green roving. Needle in place.

3. When all of the areas are covered, use the multi-needle tool to felt the roving firmly.

4. Iron both sides of the felted areas with a steam iron.

5. Using the photo as a guide, sew silver oval beads in lines that follow the lines of the felted design. Add turquoise beads in the same way. In some places sew a line of silver beads and a line of turquoise beads together. Use beading thread and a beading needle.

6. Make a 6" string of beads to attach above the buttonhole panel like this: With the doubled thread in the needle, secure on the wrong side of the jacket and come through to the front. String on turquoise beads and silver beads to make a 6" strand. Skip the last bead, go back through the rest, pull tight, and secure again on the wrong side. ❖

Colorful Strands Cardigan

This woven wool design is just right for those who like something different but not sparkly. Loosely woven fabric pieces provide the base for the felted embellishments and the added pocket. The sweater we used does not have buttons and buttonholes. If your sweater has buttons, you may want to change them to match or coordinate with the weaving.

SUPPLIES

- Unlined cardigan sweater
- Wool roving – purple teal, gray
- 1 skein loosely spun chunky wool yarn, variegated *or* skeins of different colors of chunky wool
- Sewing thread to match sweater

TOOLS

- Foam pad, 12" x 18"
- Multi-needle tool and felting needles
- Single felting needle
- Sewing needle

INSTRUCTIONS

Create the Felted Pieces:

1. Start by making two pieces of loosely woven and needled felted fabric in the following sizes for the back and front: 4" x 32", 4" x 12". Tear the wool roving into thick pieces to cover the area. Weave the roving loosely rather than just layering. Needle each piece just enough to hold it together. You want a loose piece, not a compact piece.
2. Make a more tightly needled piece of fabric for the pocket measuring 7" x 7".

Place Two Pieces of Fabric:

1. Place the sweater right side up with the foam pad under the upper back area of the sweater. (This is the area you will work on first.) Lay the 4" x 32" piece of fabric on the upper back of the sweater. Place it at an angle from the center back, up over the right shoulder, and down the right front side. Use the photo as a guide.
2. Pin the fabric piece at the shoulder to hold it securely while you work the back.
3. Needle slightly here and there to hold the woven piece in place.
4. Position the 4" x 12" piece to fill in the area on the left back shoulder. Needle this piece to hold it in place.

Add Yarn on the Back:

1. Lay horizontal strands of yarn across the woven pieces of fabric, placing the strands 1" to 1½" apart. Add interest by laying these strands irregularly and allowing the yarn to create a loop or swirl occasionally. Lightly needle the strands in place with a felting needle.
2. When the horizontal lines are secured, the next step is to weave the vertical pieces through. Space them as you did the horizontal yarn pieces; again, it will be more interesting if you let the lines fall irregularly. Because the horizontal yarns were not needled firmly, you'll find it's easy to lift them to slip under the vertical yarns as you weave. To create a gentle fringe, leave the bottom ends of the vertical pieces a bit longer and don't needle them – allow them to hang loose.
3. When all the vertical yarn pieces are woven into the design, use the felting needle to go over each strand of yarn to firmly attach it. Remove the sweater from the pad.

continued on page 70.

Colorful Strands Cardigan, continued

Add Yarn on the Front:

1. Position the right front part of the sweater face up with the foam pad underneath the area where you applied the fabric. Needle the woven fabric to secure it to the sweater front.

2. Apply yarn pieces over the fabric, following the steps in the previous section of instructions and using the photo as a guide for placing the yarn. When you are pleased with the weaving, use the felting needle to firmly secure each piece of yarn.

Add the Pocket:

1. Use the remaining 7" x 7" woven piece for the pocket. Place it on the foam block.

2. Apply pieces of yarn horizontally, using the photo as a guide, and needle them in place.

3. Add vertical pieces of yarn, weaving them as you did before, and needle them firmly in place.

4. Try on your sweater to determine where on the lower left side of the sweater to place the pocket. Pin the pocket piece in place. Take off the sweater.

5. Use the sewing needle and thread to baste the pocket in place along bottom and sides.

6. Cut three or four strands of yarn 7" to 7½" long. Lay them on the right edge of the pocket and along the bottom. Needle the yarn firmly to cover the seams until attached.

7. For the left edge of the pocket, cut yarn pieces 8" to 9" long. Place them over the seam and needle in place until firmly attached, leaving the ends hanging free below the corner of the pocket. See the pocket photo. ❖

Cape of Cloud Jacket

SUPPLIES

- Unlined white wool jacket
- 1 oz. of key lime cloud
- 1 oz. of purple cloud
- 1 skein multi-color mohair yarn with metallic gold fibers (added to felted area)
- 1 skein multicolor wool yarn (added to felted area)
- 1 skein green mohair yarn (added to felted area)
- 1 skein purple fuzzy novelty yarn or multi-color novelty yarn (for chain trim on yokes)
- 1 skein purple mohair yarn (for edge trim & neck ring)
- 1 skein multi-color boucle wool yarn (for edge trim & neck ring)
- 1 skein purple eyelash yarn (for neck ring)
- 1 pkg. green seed beads, size 6
- 1 pkg. purple seed beads, size 6
- Purple beads, 6½" strand
- 5 barrel buttons (to fit buttonholes of jacket)
- Beading thread to match jacket
- Sewing thread
- Fabric adhesive

TOOLS

- Foam pad, 12" x 12" x 3"
- Multi-needle tool and 6 felting needles, 36 gauge
- Single felting needle
- Knitting needles, size 17
- Beading needle
- Sewing needle
- P crochet hook
- Iron and ironing board

An unlined boiled wool jacket provides the perfect "canvas" for an artistic combination of felted cloud colors and a variety of coordinated yarns. The yarn tassel on the back can be in the center or a few inches to one side or the other for an asymmetrical design. Crocheted chains are used to trim the edges. A knitted ring scarf provides the finishing touch.

INSTRUCTIONS

Create the Felted Area:

Here the wool cloud is needled directly to the base rather than making a fabric piece first and then attaching. Remove buttons from jacket to prevent needle breakage.

1. Place the jacket face up on the foam pad. Arrange pieces of key lime green wool cloud and purple wool cloud on the front yoke areas. Needle the wool cloud well using the needle tool. Add pieces of clouds as you needle to cover the areas completely. Vary the colors of the cloud pieces as you add on. Needle until you have created a solid firm felted piece.
2. Repeat the procedure for the back yoke area.
3. To add color variety to the felt, needle pieces of yarn into the wool felted area. First, lay the multi-color mohair yarn with metallic gold fibers over the felted areas in a meandering arrangement. Needle firmly with a single felting needle. Lay in pieces of multicolor wool and needle in. Then lay in piece of green mohair and needle in. Place these randomly to add color variations.
4. Press on the wrong side with steam iron set on the wool setting to lock the fibers in place.

Crochet Chain Trim:

1. Crochet a very long chain using three strands of novelty yarn to make the roping trim that is on the felted area. You will need a chain long enough to meander over the felted area. See "How to Crochet a Chain" in Appendix section for instructions. Leave 6" to 8" yarn tails on the end of the chain.
2. Lay the roping randomly on the front and back yokes in a pleasing design, using the photo as a guide.

Continued on page 75

Cape of Cloud Jacket, continued

3. Use a beading needle and beading thread to attach the roping every 1" to 1½". Add beads to the thread where the thread crosses the roping for sparkle and interest. (Since most novelty yarns are not wool and will not felt, the roping must be stitched on with a needle and thread.)

4. Attach the end of the crocheted roping at the lowest point of the edge of the back yoke. Tie the roping in a knot at the end of the crocheting, leaving the 6" to 8" of yarn for a tassel. Stitch securely at the knot. Add beads to some yarn strands in the tassel.

5. At the base of the tassel, stitch a cluster of beads to cover most of the tassel top.

6. Add small clusters of beads in a variety of sizes along the roping. TIP: Don't overdo this.

Edge Trim:

1. Crochet a chain with purple mohair and multi-color boucle twice the length of the jacket neck and front and bottom edge of jacket. Attach this chain with needle and thread to all jacket edges. Start at one of the side seams and continue around all edges twice.

2. Crochet chains twice the length of the measurement of the sleeve ends and pocket tops. Stitch to the sleeve ends and pocket tops as you did on the jacket edges.

Add Buttons:

1. To cover the barrel buttons, lightly apply fabric adhesive to the ends and sides of each button and wrap with multi-colored boucle yarn. Let dry completely.

2. Attach the buttons with purple mohair yarn.

Knit a Ring Scarf:

1. With the multicolor boucle, the purple mohair, and the eyelash yarns held together as one, cast on 13 stitches using size 17 knitting needles. See "How to Knit" in the Appendix section for instructions. Knit until the piece is 4" x 16". Bind off.

2. Twist one end of the scarf twice, and stitch the two ends together with needle and thread. (This twist allows the scarf to lay flat on your chest for a less bulky appearance.) Wear it like a collar around the top of the jacket as shown. ❖

Pretty Petals Jacket

This boiled wool jacket has a felted yoke of wool cloud and asymmetrical flowers made from cutout felt petals arranged around the standup collar. A variety of beads add sparkle and shine. It looks like the perfect jacket to wear to your holiday gatherings.

SUPPLIES

- Unlined red boiled wool jacket
- 1 oz. lime cloud or roving
- 1 oz. red cloud or roving
- 1 yd. red fuzzy yarn
- 200 matte red seed beads, size 6
- 6 round green beads, ½"
- 3 green disc beads, ½"
- 40 green seed beads, assorted sizes
- Red sewing thread

TOOLS

- Multi-needle tool and 6 needles, 36 gauge
- Foam pad, 12" x 12" x 3"
- Beading needle
- Sewing needle

Pattern appears on page 78.

INSTRUCTIONS

Create the Felted Areas:

1. Place the jacket, face up, on a foam pad. Place a thin layer of lime cloud on the upper yoke area of the front and back. (See the photo for wool placement – it's okay if you can see the color of the jacket through the roving.)
2. Needle the roving in place.

Make the Flower Petals:

1. Use the red cloud or roving to make a piece of ¼" thick felt fabric measuring 16" x 28". See "Making Felt Fabric" for detailed instructions.
2. From the felt fabric, cut 37 petals using the pattern provided. Vary the pieces slightly, cutting some larger and some smaller than the pattern.
3. Using the photo as a guide, place the petals around the collar of the jacket over the lime roving, needling them in place as you add them. Use the photo as a guide for placement. Make an arrangement of one layer of petals on the right front so they radiate from a central point, overlapping them. Make another arrangement on the left shoulder, radiating from a central point, overlapping and layering them.
4. At the central points from which the petals radiate, lay a small piece of red wool and felt it into place to make the flower centers.

Add the Beads:

1. Stitch red seed beads along the length of the center of some of the petals, leaving some of the petals without beads.
2. Lay a small cluster of red fuzzy yarn in each flower center. Stitch each lightly with red thread to hold it in place.
3. Stitch the round green beads on top of the red yarn in the flower centers.
4. Stitch green seed beads and green disc beads around the outer edges of the flower centers.
5. Using the tip of a needle, fluff the strands of red fuzzy yarn to fill the spaces around the beads. ❖

Petal Pattern for Jacket

Cut 37 petals in varying sizes from smaller to larger.

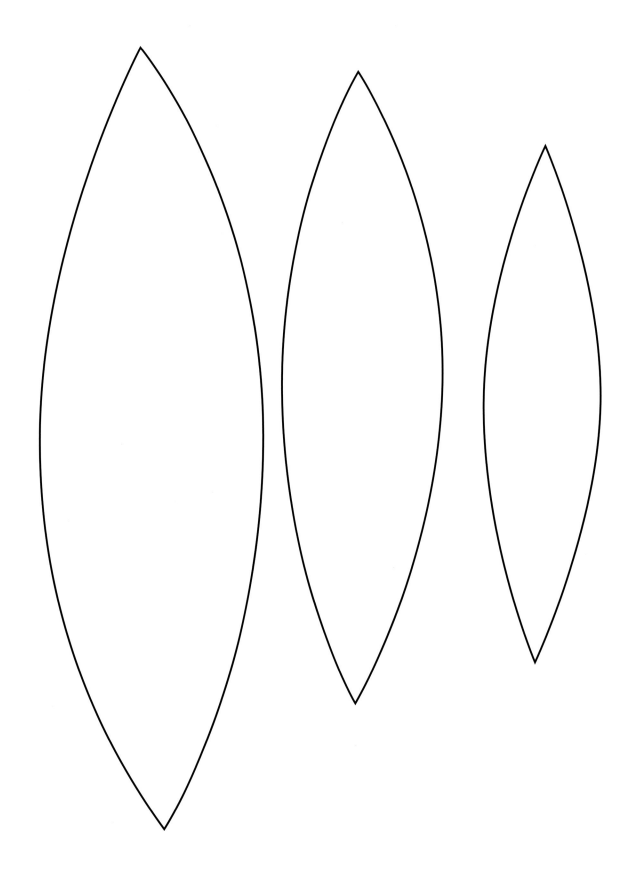

Trimmed in Style Sweater

This is a terrific project for a beginner who wants to produce an impressive, easy garment. The ivory wool yarn is felted in place as trim down front and around neckline. If you choose a sweater with buttons, you'll need to remove the buttons – felting needles can break when you hit a button. Later, you'll sew them back on.

SUPPLIES

- Black sweater (with or without buttons)
- 1 skein ivory 100% wool thick-and-thin yarn
- Thread (to sew buttons)

TOOLS

- Foam pad, 12" x 12" x 2"
- Single felting needle
- Multi-needle tool and 6 felting needles, 36 gauge
- Sewing needle
- Iron and ironing board

INSTRUCTIONS

1. Remove the buttons from the sweater if your sweater has them.
2. Lay the bottom front edge of the sweater on the foam pad. Starting at the bottom on one side and working one area at a time, arrange the yarn in a random squiggle and needle it firmly into place with a single needle. As you start needling, the yarn will be pulled into the sweater fiber.
3. Continue needling the yarn in a meandering design about 2" wide all along the front edge and back neck edge of the sweater, making loops and circles and squiggles along the sweater's edges. Use the single needle, moving the foam pad as necessary. Don't try to force the yarn into a straight line.
4. When you have finished the design, go back with the multi-needle felting tool and needle the entire area very well to lock the fibers. TIP: You'll know you have needled enough when you can see the design on the inside of the sweater.
5. Press lightly on the wrong side, using a steam iron on the wool setting. Let the sweater cool before moving to the next area. This also helps secure the fibers.
6. Sew on all the buttons. ❖

Counting Sheep Blanket Throw

This fringed herringbone wool throw takes on a charming country look with the addition of a herd of wooly sheep across one end. The needling takes only a short amount of time. Can you imagine how sweet these lambs might be bouncing across the front of a toddler's shirt or sweater front? Just adjust the size down a bit as needed.

SUPPLIES

- Woolen throw
- 1 skein ivory chunky lumpy yarn
- 1 skein lightweight dark gray yarn

TOOLS

- Foam pad, 12" x 12" x 3"
- Single felting needle, 36 gauge
- Tissue paper
- Pencil
- Iron and ironing board

Patterns appear on page 84.

INSTRUCTIONS

1. Trace the sheep patterns on tissue paper and cut out the shapes.
2. Place one end of the throw on the foam pad.
3. Place one of the tissue paper patterns on the throw where you want the first sheep to be. Using the ivory yarn and the felting needle, outline the sheep's body by tacking the yarn lightly around the pattern shape. Remove the paper.
4. With yarn, fill in the entire body area of the sheep with loops of yarn. Tack the loops down slightly by needling in place. When you are happy with the yarn placement, needle firmly to secure all the loops and the ends of the yarn.
5. Use dark gray wool yarn to shape the sheep's legs and nose, using the photograph as a guide. As with the body, tack the yarn gently until you are satisfied with the placement, then needle well to bond it to the throw.
6. Repeat the process to create additional sheep. As you finish each sheep, lift the throw carefully from the foam pad. Check the back side – when the fibers are visible on the back you can be sure you have needled enough to create a secure bond.
7. When you've finished all the sheep, heat the iron to the wool setting and use steam to press the back side of the throw, holding the iron ½" above the throw to get as much steam as possible into the wool. Then press very gently to lock the fibers in place. Allow the area to dry and cool before you move the throw; the cooling process helps secure the fibers. ❖

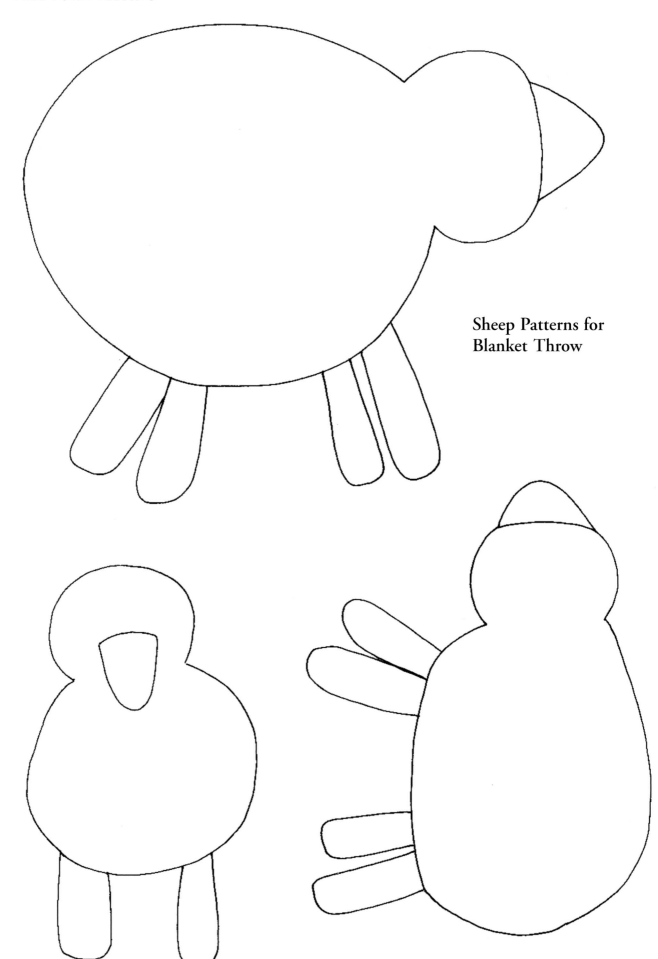

**Sheep Patterns for
Blanket Throw**

Close-up of completed sheep.

chapter 6

Making Felt Jewelry

Needle felted beads are quite simple to make, and they are so versatile you will want to make handfuls. They can be embellished in a number of ways and used as jewelry, to decorate hats or jackets, or strung together for a purse handle. Larger wool beads are lovely when used as a single button.

Making Tube Beads

Tube beads start with a felted fabric rectangle that is rolled and needled until firm, then cut.

1. Make felted fabric.

Start with a piece of wool roving the size of your hand. Use the multi-needle tool to make a loosely felted rectangle about 5" x 4" from wool roving or cloud. See "Making Felt Fabric" for detailed instructions.

2. Roll and needle.

Turn up the long edge of the felted rectangle to make a roll of felt, needling with a single needle as you make the roll.

3. Continue rolling and needling.

Continue rolling and needling until the entire rectangle has been rolled into a tube shape. Rotate and needle the roll until it is firm and round. On the roll pictured above, one end is felted firmly; the other end shows the way it looks just after the rolling is finished but before it was felted further.

4. Cut the roll.

Cut off the ends of the roll to straighten them and cut the roll into even lengths to make the tube beads. For cutting, you can use sharp scissors or a craft knife. TIPS: When using a craft knife, a new blade gives best results. Save the cutoff ends; you can use them to decorate other beads.

5. Make the holes.

To create a hole in the felt bead, run a felting needle through the center of the bead.

Making Round Beads

To make a round felted bead, take a small amount of wool and squeeze it tightly in your hand. This gives you a feel for how big the bead will be once it is felted. Add more fibers for a larger bead, or take some away for a smaller bead. When you think the amount is right, pull the fibers gently to determine their direction.

1. Begin rolling.

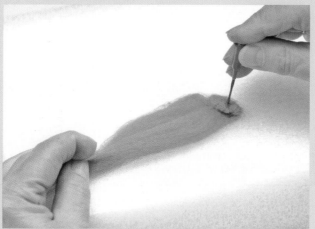

Lay your clump of wool on a foam pad and begin rolling and pinching at one end.

2. Needle to form the bead.

When half of the wool piece is rolled tight, start needling the bead to form a ball. Be careful not to poke your fingers when working with such a small item.

3. Continue to needle and turn.

Needle and turn the bead as you work until it is well formed and quite firm. The longer you needle the felt, the stronger and firmer the bead will be. Creating beads of a consistent size takes practice. Until you have more experience, you may find it necessary to make several extra beads in order to have three or five of uniform size.

An assortment of finished beads in various colors and sizes. Some are made with one color of wool; others are blends of colors. Some are decorated with pencil roving, which is narrow like yarn but not spun. It can be tacked in place with a felting needle to form designs and then felted in place.

Winter Wardrobe Necklace

Make a strand of beads to compliment your wooly winter clothes. A decorated central barrel bead is surrounded by symmetrical arrangements of felted round beads and silver beads. Here, we've used silver spacers and round beads to embellish the barrel bead. For a different look, designs made with pencil roving or wool scraps of other colors could be used.

SUPPLIES
- Green wool roving
- 14 silver tube beads, 1" long
- 16 silver disc beads
- 8 silver spacer beads
- Silver spacer beads, 6mm (to decorate the barrel bead)
- Silver round beads, 3mm (to decorate the barrel bead)
- Green beading thread, size G
- Silver toggle clasp
- Clear nail polish

TOOLS
- Felting needle
- Foam block
- Beading needle

INSTRUCTIONS
1. Create eight round felted beads approximately ¾" in diameter and one barrel-shaped bead approximately 1" in diameter from green wool roving. See "Making Round Beads" for detailed instructions.
2. Arrange the beads in a row, with the barrel bead at the center and four pairs of closely matched round beads on either side to determine the best placement for the necklace.
3. Thread the beading needle with doubled beading thread and knot onto one side of the toggle closure. String a silver spacer, a silver tube bead, a silver spacer, a silver tube bead, a silver spacer, a silver tube bead, and a silver spacer.
4. Add a round felted bead, a disc bead, a tube bead, and a disc bead. Repeat this sequence three times.
5. Add the barrel bead. Reverse the sequence in step 4, then the sequence in step 2. Tie off the

thread on the other side of the toggle closure.
6. Seal the knots with clear nail polish. Let dry.
7. Embellish the barrel bead with a row of 6mm spacers topped by 3mm round beads. Using a beading needle and thread, go through both beads, then back though the spacer. (The small round bead holds the spacer in place.) ❖

Amulet Bag

You can wear this small bag around your neck as a necklace or carry it as a tiny handbag. Black craft felt is used as a base for felting. Make it just the right size for holding a tube of lipstick or the essential credit card.

SUPPLIES

- Black craft felt, 11" x 4½"
- Wool cloud
- 32" heavy gold chain
- 1 gold jump ring
- Gold charm
- Black sewing thread

TOOLS

- Single felting needle
- Foam block
- Iron and ironing board

INSTRUCTIONS

1. Place the black craft felt piece on the foam block. Spread part of the wool cloud evenly over the craft felt and needle felt the cloud to the craft felt. This process is like adding wool to a garment – see the section on "Free Form Felting" for details.
2. Remove the piece from the foam block. Iron with a steam iron to secure the fibers.
3. Place the felted piece on your work surface with the roving side down. Fold up 4" of felt to make the bottom part of the amulet bag. Needle the seams on both sides until seams are secure.
4. Turn down the felt at the top 2" to make the flap. To make a casing for the chain along the top edge, needle with the single needle ½" from the top edge.
5. Thread the chain through the casing and connect the ends with a jump ring. (You can hide this ring in the casing.)
6. Make a cut diagonally across the bottom of the flap, removing a triangular piece of felt. Reposition the cutoff piece vertically on the flap, lining up the wide end of the triangle with the bottom of the bag. Needle the cutoff piece to the flap to make the flap extension.
7. Sew a charm on the flap extension with black thread. ❖

Multi-Strand Necklace

This colorful necklace alternates matte finish wooly tube beads and a variety of shiny glass and silver beads. For best results, select glass and silver beads whose diameters match those of the tube beads.

SUPPLIES

- Multiple colors of wool roving
- Three-hole silver clasp
- 51 multi-colored glass beads, various sizes and shapes
- 15 small and large silver beads
- Green beading thread, size G
- Clear nail polish

TOOLS

- Multi-needle tool
- Single felting needle
- Beading needle

INSTRUCTIONS

1. With various colors of wool roving make 58 felt tube beads, each approximately 1" long. See "Making Tube Beads" at the beginning of this section. The diameters of the beads will vary – that's good.
2. Cut about three yards of beading thread and thread the beading needle with doubled thread. Tie on one side of the clasp. Make several knots.
3. Start stringing beads with one small silver bead. Then add alternating felt beads and glass or silver beads until you have a 29" strand. End with one small silver bead. Tie off the thread on the other side of the clasp.
4. Make two more 29" strands the same way.
5. Seal all the knots with clear nail polish. Let dry. ❖

Diamond Felted Bracelet

This bracelet combines needle felted diamonds, felted tube beads, and silver beads. The tube beads can be any color you like. See "Making Tube Beads" at the beginning of this section for instructions.

SUPPLIES

- Turquoise craft felt, 9" x 12"
- Wool roving – Turquoise, teal
- 6 felted tube beads, ¾" long – Assorted colors
- 6 silver flower shaped spacer beads
- 6 silver round beads, 3mm
- Teal pearl cotton
- Blue beading thread, size B
- Large snap

TOOLS

- Sewing needle
- Beading needle
- Scissors
- Ruler
- Foam pad
- Multi-needle tool
- Sewing needle
- Single felting needle

INSTRUCTIONS

1. Cut six 1¼" squares of turquoise craft felt.
2. From turquoise roving and teal roving, make one felted fabric rectangle 3¾" x 1¼" from each color.
3. Cut the felted fabric pieces into 1¼" squares – three turquoise squares and three teal squares.
4. Sew the felted squares to the craft felt squares with pearl cotton, using a blanket stitch.
5. Sew the points of the squares together, overlapping them slightly, forming a row of diamond shapes.
6. Sew silver beads where the diamonds overlap: With a beading needle threaded with beading thread, come from the back to the front at the point. Put on one spacer bead and one round bead. Go back through the spacer bead and the felt. Tie off. Repeat where all the points meet.
7. Sew one felted ¾" tube bead at the center of each diamond shape.
8. Try on the bracelet to determine the placement of the snap. Sew half the snap on each end. ❖

Fashion Circles Pendant Necklace

One felted bullseye bead takes a solo turn on pendant wire. It's decorated with a single gold bead.

SUPPLIES

- Gold wire necklace
- 1 gold melon bead, 9mm
- 2 gold tube beads, ¼"
- 1 gold head pin
- 6 colors of roving – Turquoise, lime green, magenta, green, purple, teal

TOOLS

- Wire cutters
- Roundnose pliers
- Single felting needle
- Foam block
- Craft knife

INSTRUCTIONS

1. Following the instructions for "Making Round Beads" earlier in this section, make a small, firm round bead from turquoise roving.
2. Add the other colors of roving, one at a time, to make the layers of the bullseye. Use lime green, then magenta, then green, then purple, then teal, ending with a second layer of turquoise roving. Use enough roving to make each layer so the color underneath does not show.
3. Continue needling the bead until it is round and firm, about 1¼" in diameter.
4. Cut off one end of the bead, using a sharp craft knife. To make the bullseye bead, cut a ¼" wide slice from the middle of the round bead. Save the extra pieces of the round bead – they can be cut and used to make other beads.

5. With the felting needle, make a vertical hole through the slice. See the photo for placement.
6. Place the 9mm gold bead on the head pin. Insert the head pin through the hole in the slice. Using roundnose pliers, make a loop at the top of the head pin. Trim excess wire with the cutters.
7. On the wire necklace, place one tube bead, the pendant, and the other tube bead. ❖

Memory Wire Bracelets

Coiled memory wire holds its shape and snaps back when expanded and released so it makes a great base for this trio of colorful bracelets. There are no holes in the tube beads – we used the felting needle to poke a hole for the wire to go through to make stringing them easier. Be sure to bend the felt beads as you push them onto the memory wire to avoid having the wire poke through the side of the bead.

Red & Gold Bracelet

This bracelet is a variation of the "Red & Silver Bracelet." Make it just like the silver bracelet, substituting gold beads for the silver. Gold pencil roving spirals around the tube beads. Firmly attach the pencil roving in place on the tube beads by needling with a single needle.

Turquoise & Gold Bracelet

SUPPLIES
- Turquoise wool roving
- 3 silver-lined round turquoise beads, 10mm
- 4 silver-lined oval turquoise beads, 14mm
- 9 gold disc beads, 11mm
- 4 gold round beads, 9mm
- 7 gold oval beads, 10mm x 8mm
- 1 gold heart charm
- Memory wire

TOOLS
- Roundnose pliers
- Wire cutters
- Foam pad
- Single felting needle
- Multi-needle tool and felting needles

INSTRUCTIONS
1. From turquoise roving, make 10 felted tube beads each ½" long. Follow the instructions for "Making Tube Beads" at the beginning of this section.
2. With roundnose pliers, make a loop at one end of the memory wire.
3. String on a gold disc bead, a gold oval bead, a felt bead, a gold disc bead, and a felt bead. Reserve a gold oval bead and a gold disc bead.
4. Add a gold bead, a turquoise bead (round or oval), a gold bead, and a felt bead. Repeat this sequence six times.
5. Add the reserved gold oval bead and gold disc bead.
6. Trim the excess wire. Make a loop on the end. Attach the charm. TIP: To cut memory wire, score the wire with wire cutters, then bend the wire back and forth until it breaks. ❖

Red & Silver Bracelet

SUPPLIES
- Red variegated roving
- 20 silver spacer beads, 7mm
- 3 round silver beads, 10mm
- 2 bicone silver beads, 9mm
- 2 bicone silver beads, 7mm
- Memory wire

TOOLS
- Roundnose pliers
- Wire cutters
- Foam pad
- Single felting needle
- Multi-needle tool and felting needles

INSTRUCTIONS
1. From the variegated red roving, make four felted beads, each 2½" long. Follow the instructions for "Making Tube Beads" at the beginning of this section.
2. With roundnose pliers make a loop in one end of the memory wire.
3. Add two spacer beads, a 7mm bicone, two spacer beads, and a 9mm bicone bead. Add one felted bead.
4. Add two spacer beads, one round bead, two spacer beads, and one felted bead. Repeat this sequence two times.
5. Add a 9mm bicone bead, two spacer beads, a 7mm bicone, and two spacer beads.
6. Cut excess wire and form a loop at the end with round-nose pliers. TIP: To cut memory wire, score the wire with wire cutters, then bend the wire back and forth until it breaks. ❖

Beaded Fantasy Bracelet

A strip of felt fabric is needled to create a backing for this charming bracelet. Fanciful yarn and an array of glass beads decorate the front of the felt piece to create one-of-a-kind art jewelry. Tailor the colors to match your outfit, and make one for every color of outfit. These are quick to create and make wonderful gifts for your friends.

SUPPLIES

- ⅛ oz. royal blue roving
- 4 assorted yarns in 2-yd. lengths
- 24" silver wire, 18 gauge
- Assorted blue and black glass beads, various sizes
- 1 pkg. blue seed beads, size 6
- Blue beading thread (to match fabric)

TOOLS

- Single felting needle
- Multi-needle tool and 6 needles, 36 gauge
- P crochet hook
- Needlenose pliers
- Wire cutters
- Beading needle
- Straight pins
- Foam pad

INSTRUCTIONS

1. From royal blue roving, needle felt a strip of fabric 1" x 7" or long enough to fit around wrist, minus 1". (Photo 1)
2. Using the four yarn pieces as one, crochet a chain 7" long. See "How to Crochet a Chain" in Appendix section for instructions. (Photo 2)
3. Make a loop on one end of the silver wire. Using needlenose pliers, bend the wire back and forth, making bends every 1" to 1½" to make a wire frame for the felted fabric strip. Leave enough wire to make a hook on the other end. (Photo 3) Form to fit your wrist. Form the hook on the end.
4. Lay the crocheted chain on top of felted fabric. Stitch in place with a needle and matching thread.
5. Weave the felt strip through the bent wire frame. (Photo 4)
6. Stitch the blue and black glass beads to the bracelet – larger ones first – with a needle and thread, stitching through the wire frame of bracelet and placing the beads every ¾" to 1". Stitch smaller beads around the larger beads. Fill in around the assorted beads with blue seed beads.
7. Make three strands of beads on the end near the loop like this: Knot the thread in the back. Come to the front and string on six seed beads, one larger bead, and one seed bead. Skipping the last bead, bring the thread back through the others. Knot off. Repeat to make two more strands. ❖

Photo 1 – Felting the fabric strip.

Photo 2 – Crocheting the chain.

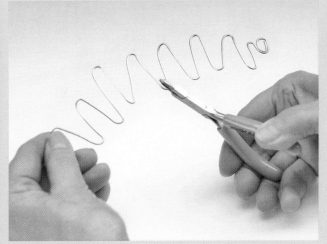

Photo 3 – Forming the wire frame of the bracelet.

Photo 4 – Weaving the felt strip through the wire frame.

Finished Bracelet

Tropical Bird Pin

This cheerful fellow is simple to make and a delight to wear. It would make a great gift for a friend who loves compliments.

SUPPLIES

- ½ oz. gray wool roving or cloud
- Small bits of yellow, orange, and olive green wool roving or cloud
- 3 black seed beads
- Green seed beads
- Orange seed beads
- 2 cone-shaped amber beads (for the "feet")
- 7" black wire, 24 gauge
- Beading thread (to match wool)
- Pin back, 1¼"

TOOLS

- Foam pad, 6" x 6" x 3"
- Single felting needle
- Beading needle

The bird's body, a tail feather, and other supplies.

INSTRUCTIONS

Make the Felted Shapes:

1. Take a small handful of gray wool. Determine the direction of the fibers. Working from one end of the fibers, roll and pinch them to form a small tubular shape. Needle the bundle, rolling as you work. The goal is a soft but firm C-shape about 2½" long.

2. Make five green tail feathers, using the same technique used to make the body, but make the feathers smaller and flatter than the body piece. Work gently to get a slight point on both ends of each feather. Needle a line down the center of each tail feather for definition.

3. Make an orange wing, using the same technique, but make it wider than the tail feathers. One end of the wing is rounded; the other end has a gentle point. When the wing is sufficiently felted, needle one long edge to form scallops. (This scalloped edge will be the bottom of the wing.)

4. For the beak, take a small bit of yellow wool and roll and pinch it as you needle. Be very careful of your fingers! Work one end to a point; the other end fatter and fuzzy.

Assemble:

1. When the beak is the size and shape you want, place the fatter end behind the gray body, using the photo as a guide for placement. Needle firmly into place on the back. TIP: By needling a bit on the front, you can get the bill to look quite natural.

2. Decide how you wish to place the tail feathers – some should be placed on top of the body and others under-neath. When the arrangement pleases you, needle them to the body.

3. Sew the wing on the body with a needle and thread, using the photo as a guide.

4. Sew a cluster of orange seed beads to cover the stitching on the wing.

5. Stitch a line of green seed beads at the base of each tail feather. TIPS: Don't try to make them all the same. Add additional beads for sparkle and to break up the straight line.

6. Sew one black seed bead for the eye.

7. Make the bird's legs by placing orange and green seed beads on the wire. Put a cone-shaped bead on each end, with the wide end towards the end of the wire. Finish each end with a black seed bead. Coil the wire ends to secure. Bend the wire in half to make the two legs and stitch to the back of the body, using the photo as a guide for placement. ❖

Embellished Bead Necklaces

Embroidery and beading are two wonderful ways to embellish felted beads. The necklaces on the following pages provide two examples. The basic steps are the same for both necklaces. The same techniques could be used to create a bracelet – just make the felt beads a bit smaller.

Pictured on pages 100 and 101.

BASIC SUPPLIES
- Small amounts of wool roving or cloud
- Colorful threads *or* lightweight yarns (for embroidery)
- Assorted beads and/or pearls in coordinating colors
- Clear beading thread
- *Optional:* Necklace clasp

BASIC TOOLS
- Foam pad, 6" x 6" x 3"
- Single felting needles
- Sewing needle

BASIC INSTRUCTIONS

Make the Beads:

Make three round beads that are the same size and color, following the instructions for "Making Round Beads" that appear at the beginning of this section. Needle and turn each bead as you work until it is well-formed and quite firm. *Note:* Consistent size takes practice. You may need to make a number of beads to have three of uniform size.

Decorate the beads with any of the following techniques.

Embellish the Beads with Embroidery:

Stitch a small design on the bead – a simple chain stitch is a good choice. Use tinier stitches on very small beads, and slightly larger ones on medium to large beads. TIP: To avoid using knots when embroidering,

Continued on next page

Embellished Bead Necklaces, continued

pull the floss through the bead just until the tail disappears into the wool. Turn the needle around and go straight back through the bead to anchor the thread, then begin stitching your design.

Use the *outline stitch* to make a line of stitches that bends and curves around the bead. Bring the threaded needle from the center of the bead at the point where you want to begin the stitching. Working on the surface of the bead, push the needle in about ¼" to the right and come up between the two points of your thread. Keeping the thread above the last stitch, go into the bead for the second stitch about ¼" from where the thread last came out. This ensures stitches of equal length.

Beaded Beads:

Sew individual beads, bead clusters, or rows of beads to your felted beads. Ropes of tiny beads, made by stringing beads on beading thread and wrapping them around the felted bead, are especially nice. As you embroider, you could add beads here and there for sparkle, or add the beads after the embroidery is complete.

Thread-wrapped Beads:

You can wrap felted beads with colored threads or thin yarn. Use small stitches to hold the threads in place as needed. If you use wool yarn, you can attach it by felting with a single felting needle. Metallic threads add glitz and sparkle.

Assemble the Necklace:

To make a necklace, combine the wool beads with pearls or beads made of painted wood, metal, gemstones, or glass. Choose beads in colors and sizes to complement the wool beads. String them on clear beading thread. You can add a toggle or hook and eye closure or make the necklace long enough to go over your head (so you don't need a clasp). *Option:* Add a tassel of yarn or beads to the center bead. String beaded tassels on beading thread. ❖

Lavender & Blue Necklace

Felted beads are wrapped with yarn, fine metallic thread, and strings of beads. Seed beads in a narrow palette of colors (lavender, blue, gold, and pearl) are strung with natural pearls and assorted wooden and metal beads in the same palette of colors. There's no clasp. A beaded tassel with a different bead on the end of each strand provides the finishing touch.

Red & White Necklace

White felted beads are decorated with red thread embroidery – two with straight lines, one with curvy lines and beads. Painted beads and lustrous pearls are an unlikely, but effective, combination. The necklace has a hook-and-eye clasp and a bright red crocheted thread tassel.

chapter 7

Making Felted Embellishmens

Embellishments are the elements that give a garment personality. They show others that you enjoy something out of the ordinary and express your style – be it classic, offbeat, wild and flashy, or neat and matching, it is who you are.

Use this chapter to learn the basics, and let our ideas help you see the possibilities. Gather inspiration where you find it – from nature, photos in magazines, or a cartoon figure. You can create nearly anything you can imagine using needle felting. Three-dimensional pieces can be easily and quickly made from leftover bits of wool and used to enhance clothing, hats, bags, wall hangings, and baskets.

When making a hat, for example, simply set aside a handful of wool, finishing the hat with just a bit less then the full 4 ounces, and use that handful of wool to make a rose or a bird's tail feathers for another project. As you practice making some of these simple embellishments, you will see how little it actually takes (in materials and time) to produce an embellishment that makes something simple really special.

Flowers & Leaves

Creating flowers with needle felting is quick and easy, whether the flowers are realistic or fantastic. All these flowers require the same supplies and tools: scraps of roving and/or cloud, the multi-needle tool, a single felting needle, a foam pad, and fabric adhesive.

The fabric for the shapes should be thin enough to roll gently, but not so thin that you can see through it. Fabric strength is not an issue when making most embellishments – they don't have to support weight like a handbag does or be as durable as a garment.

The most difficult thing about making flowers is learning to make petals that are uniform in size, but with a bit of practice, you will! With a rose, same-size petals are not an issue so try it first.

ROSE

It is possible to make roses of any size you wish by altering the size of the petals you form. Experiment with color combinations as well (Who says a rose's petals have to all be one color?) To make a rosebud, simply use fewer petals.

1. Make the petals.

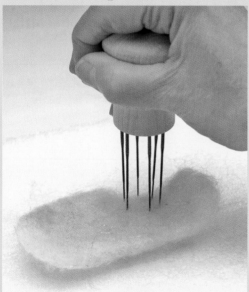

Using a small piece of wool, felt two oval shapes about 2" x 1". Make two more ovals of the same thickness, each 1½" x 3". Make another oval 1½" x 4". Use the multi-needle tool and work on the foam pad.

2. Begin forming the rose.

Take one 2" x 1" petal and roll it into a loose tube that you pinch on one end.

3. Add a second petal.

Take the second 2" x 1" petal, placing the center of it across the seam of the first. Pinch and gather it around the base of the first petal.

4. Needle.

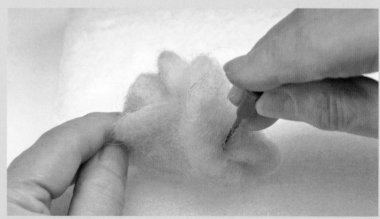

Needle the bottom area only with the single felting needle to hold the pieces together. Continue to add petals, with the largest added last. As you shape the rose, needle some petals up their sides to help hold the shape you desire. Sometimes the edges of a petal must be needled so they will keep their shape.

TRUMPET FLOWER

This flower is the classic horn shape, like a morning glory. Trumpet flowers are very simple and may be used alone or as part of a cluster. In its simplest form, this flower is made from a single petal that is rolled and needled on one end and on one side.

1. Make the petal.

Working with the multi-needle tool on the foam pad, make a half-circle petal that's finished on the rounded edge and fuzzy on the straight edge.

2. Add a second color.

Lightly needle fan-shaped rays of a second color over the first. This gives you a flower with a colored throat.

3. Roll the shape.

Roll the felted piece to make the funnel shape. Needle the fuzzy side with a single needle until the seam doesn't show.

Trumpet Flower Variations:

• Trumpet Flower with a Center

Trumpet flowers look wonderful with a center decoration. Wrap a great novelty yarn with some sparkle loosely around two or three fingers. Gently remove it from your fingers, tie the center, snip the ends, and attach it inside the trumpet. Trim the fluffy ends to the length that looks best.

• Calla Lily

A calla lily is a simple trumpet. Make one part of the half-circle a bit thicker with a strong edge. As you form the trumpet, overlap the more finished edge to give the lily its distinctive shape. For the center, make a well-needled yellow tube and anchor it inside the lily.

LEAVES

A needle felted leaf is a variation of a flower petal. Using the wool of your choice, felt a teardrop or a longer blade-like shape. Needle it well, and then needle a line down the center of the leaf to make the center vein. After you've made a few, you'll find it's easy to make a leaf that has more shape, such as a grape or maple leaf. The way you use the needle to push and poke the wool can change the shape quickly – experiment to see just what the needle will do!

Putting a thin strip of another color down the center defines the vein. Use a darker or lighter shade of the leaf color for a natural look or use a contrasting color to add drama or fantasy.

Flowers & Leaves, continued

Five-petal Posy

This type of flower takes the most patience and practice – making five petals that are consistent in size is hard.

Needle a small bit of wool to form a rounded teardrop shape. Do this five times. Lay the first petal on the foam pad with the pointed end toward the flower center. Lay the next one slightly overlapping the first. Needle them at the center to secure, and continue with the remaining petals. Adjust as needed, then needle them firmly together.

To make a flower center, needle tiny balls of another color to cluster at the center. (See "Making Round Beads" in the jewelry section.) Secure them with a dab of fabric adhesive. The adhesive will dry clear and remain flexible so your flower won't feel stiff. These tiny balls don't have enough loose fibers to unite them to other pieces; fabric adhesive solves the problem nicely.

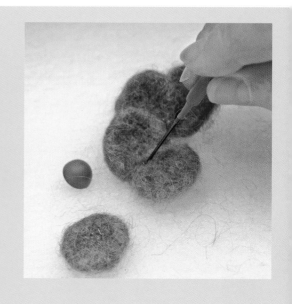

Fall Fantasy Flower

Wear this shaped flower pin on your coat, a sweater, or a hat or attach it to your handbag. The heathered colors of the wool cloud recall the shades of autumn leaves.

SUPPLIES

- ⅛ oz. red-orange cloud
- ¹⁄₁₆ oz. olive green cloud
- 4" eyelash yarn
- Pin back, 1½"
- Matching sewing thread

TOOLS

- Multi-needle tool and felting needles
- Single felting needle, 36 gauge
- Foam pad, 6" x 6" x 2"
- Sewing needle

Pattern appears on page 107.

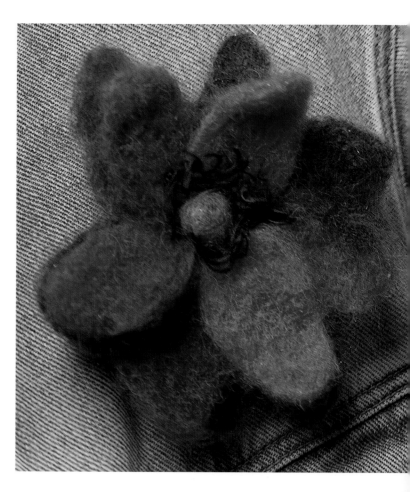

INSTRUCTIONS

Make the Pieces:

1. Using the pattern provided as a guide for the shape, needle felt four petals from red-orange cloud. See "Making Felt Fabric" for detailed instructions.

2. Needle felt two petals from olive green cloud, using the pattern provided.

3. Make a ¾" round bead from red-orange cloud. See "Making Round Beads" for instructions.

4. Working one petal at a time, twist the petal at the center, making a complete revolution. Needle gently in the center to hold the shape. (Photo 1). Repeat the process on all six petals.

Assemble:

1. Stitch through the center of one twisted red-orange petal with a needle and thread. (Photo 2) Wrap the thread twice, pull tightly around center of the petal, and knot the thread.

2. Lay one green petal on top of the red-orange petal. Stitch through the center of the green petal. Wrap the thread tightly around the centers of both petals and knot.

3. Using the same technique, add the second green petal (Photo 3) and the remaining red-orange petals.

4. Stitch black eyelash yarn in the center of the flower, using a needle and thread.

5. Stitch the felted round bead at the center of the black eyelash yarn.

6. Sew the pin back to the back of the flower.

7. Shape the flower petals with your fingers to turn them upward at the tips. ❖

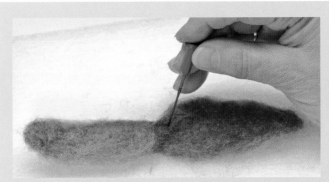

Photo 1 – Needling a petal after twisting the center.

Photo 2 – Stitching the twisted petal center with needle and thread.

Photo 3 – Assembling the petals by sewing them together at the centers.

Petal Pattern
for Flower

Making Faces

Fanciful faces are a great addition to a basket or a handbag.
They can be personalized by changing the colors or trims. The
faces are created in layers. The areas that need to be fuller are
padded with additional wool and needled to shape.

SUPPLIES

• 2 oz. pale peach roving or cloud (for face)

• Small bits of dark roving (for eyes and hair)

• Coral roving (for trimming)

• Small amount of yarn (for trimming)

• Sewing thread

TOOLS

• Foam pad, 6" x 6" x 3"

• Multi-needle tool

• Single felting needle

• Sewing needle

Instructions begin on page 110.

Making Faces, continued

INSTRUCTIONS

Face Base:

1. For the face shape, make a stack of fibers with layers of fibers placed both horizontally and vertically. The stack should be about the size of the palm of your hand and 1" to 2" thick. Tuck under the edges. Begin needling with the multi-needle tool. (Photo 1)

2. Needle to make a fairly firm piece about ¾" thick that looks like a fat, peachy hamburger. (Photo 2) Set aside.

Nose:

3. For the nose, pull a wad of wool out and squeeze it to judge the size it will be when needled. (The nose should be larger than normal to add character to the face.) When the size is right, align the fibers and begin rolling the wool, tucking in the ends as you go. When you have rolled about half the wool, begin needling. Needle until the cylinder holds its shape.

4. Put the nose on the face. Needle to attach and shape the nose. The bridge (top) is narrower and flattens onto the forehead; the nostrils end is broader and rounded. When the sides of the nose are shaped, poke upward into the end to form the nostrils. This takes time and patience. (Photo 3)

Cheeks:

5. To puff the cheeks, roll some fibers in a loose bundle and position on the face. Shape as you needle to build up the contours of the face.

Eyes:

6. Add bits of dark wool near the bridge of the nose to form the eyes. Try to keep them the same size.

Lips:

7. Shape the lips by creating two small tubular pieces of peach wool like the larger one you made for the nose. Position the tightly rolled tubes and needle to the face, shaping the tubes to form the lips. Use the photo on the opposite page as a guide. (Oversized lips make the face more comical and fun.)

8. If needed, puff up the chin to make the lips look appropriate. TIP: If you are not certain, make a small puff (like you did for the cheeks) and see if it looks good. You can always remove it if you don't like it.

Hair:

9. Place dark wool for the hair around the face, needling as you go. (Photo 4)

10. Needle tiny flowers to add to the hair. See "Making Flowers & Leaves" for instructions.

Finish:

11. Needle a shape from the coral wool to make a collar. Make a small pom-pom from yarn. Stitch to the bottom of the face, using the photo as a guide.

12. Sew the finished face on the side of a basket. ❖

Photo 1 – Beginning to needle the base piece for the face.

Photo 2 – The base piece for the face should be the size and shape of a fat, peachy hamburger.

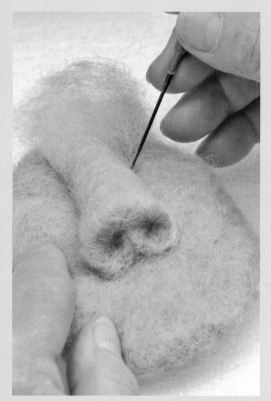

Photo 3 – Adding the nose.

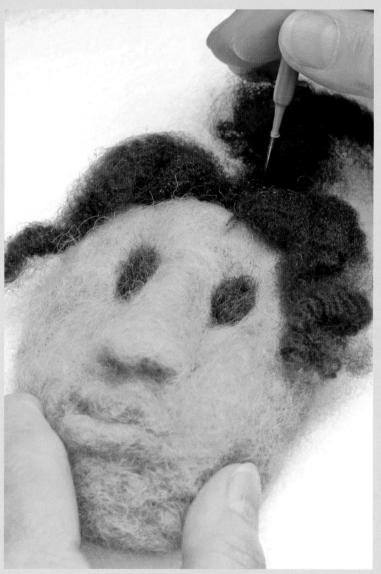

Photo 4 – Attaching the hair.

Silk & Sparkle Embellished Hat

A simple hat can be taken "over the top" using an assortment of fibers and findings. Felted beads, silk cocoons and rods, and metallic yarn are arranged in an artful cluster and trimmed with beads and a finding to decorate a simple hat.

SUPPLIES

- Wool or felt hat
- ½ oz. wool cloud
- 2 silk rods
- 3 silk cocoons
- 6 ft. heavily textured yarn
- 6 ft. sparkly metallic yarn
- 1 fancy button-type finding
- Matching beading thread
- Glass beads, various sizes in coordinating colors

TOOLS

- Foam pad, 6" x 6"x 2"
- Beading needle
- Single felting needle

Pictured clockwise from top left: Wool cloud, textured yarn, one silk rod, button-type finding, sparkly yarn, silk cocoons, beads, one silk rod

INSTRUCTIONS

1. Needle felt the textured yarn around the base of the brim to make a hat band. Leave an open space on the side where you will be adding the embellishment cluster.

2. From wool cloud, make three round beads, one ¾", one 1", and one 1¼" in diameter. See "Making Round Beads" for detailed instructions.

3. Stitch two silk rods to the side of the hat with a needle and thread.

4. Place the large finding on top of the silk rods in the center of the design area. Sew the ¾" felted bead in the center of the finding.

5. Sew the 1¼" felted bead at 1 o'clock and the 1" felted bead at 5 o'clock.

6. Stitch one silk cocoon at 4 o'clock, one at 8 o'clock, and one at 10 o'clock.

7. Cut the metallic yarn into four 16" lengths. Wrap each length around four fingers, slip the yarn off your fingers, and secure at the center to make four mini pom-poms. Stitch these at 1 o'clock, 5 o'clock, 7 o'clock, and 10 o'clock.

8. Stitch the glass beads on the cocoons and wool beads. Stitch additional beads around the design. See the photo for placement ideas. ❖

How to Crochet a Chain

We use crocheted chains to wrap purse handles and to make trims that combine various yarns. Here's how to crochet a chain:

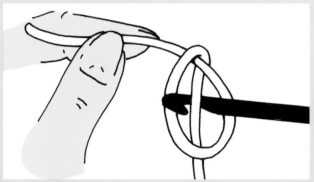

Fig. 1 – Loop the yarn around the crochet hook to make a slip knot about 4" from the end of the yarn.

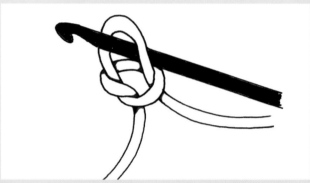

Fig. 2 – Pull the yarn to tighten with the loop over the hook.

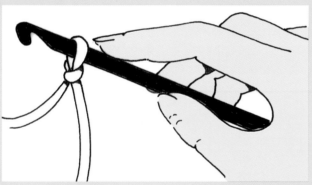

Fig. 3 – Hold the hook in your right hand between the thumb and third index finger with your index finger near the tip of the hook.

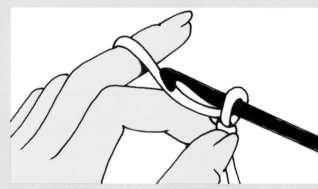

Fig. 4 – Hold the base of the slip knot with the thumb and index finger of your left hand, threading the yarn over the third finger and through the remaining fingers of your left hand.

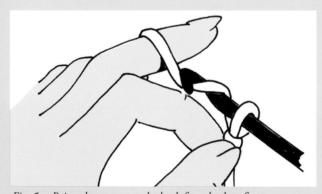

Fig. 5 – Bring the yarn over the hook from back to front.

Fig. 6 – Pull the hook through the loop of the slip knot. You have just made one chain stitch. Repeat to continue.

How to Knit

CASTING ON

Knitting starts with a row of stitches on one needle. Follow Figures 1 through 9 to **cast on**. You'll need about 1" of yarn for each stitch. If you need to make 15 stitches, for example, pull out 16" to 18" of yarn from the skein.

Making the First Stitch

Make a loop on one knitting needle, following the steps in Figures 1 through 4. This is your first stitch.

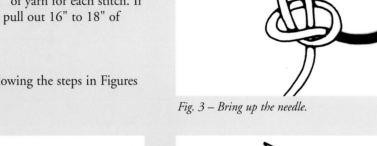

Fig. 3 – Bring up the needle.

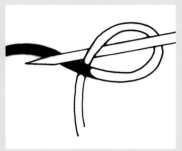

Fig. 1 – Loop the yarn around the needle.

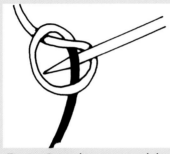

Fig. 2 – Bring the yarn around the loop.

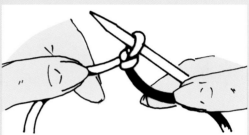

Fig. 4 – Pull the yarn.

Casting on the First Row

Figures 5 through 9 shows how to make the rest of the stitches for the first row.

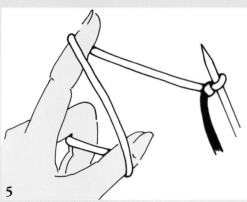

5

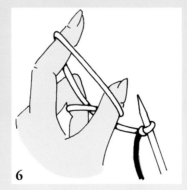

6

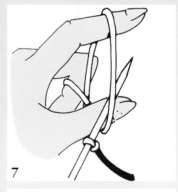

7

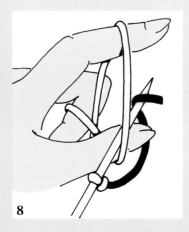

8

9

Fig. 5 – Hold the needle with the stitch in your right hand and the yarn from the skein in your left.

Fig. 6. – Make a loop of yarn with your left hand.

Fig. 7 – Put the needle into the loop.

Fig. 8 – Catch the tail to your right and pull it through the loop in your left hand.

Fig. 9 – Work the ends of the yarn to snug the yarn onto the needle. (You don't want it tight – just loosely snug.) Repeat the process in Figures 5 through 9 until you have made the number of stitches you need.

How to Knit, continued

THE KNIT STITCH

When you have finished casting on, you can begin to knit.

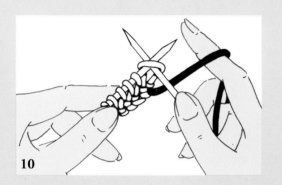

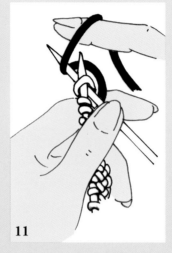

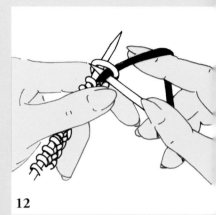

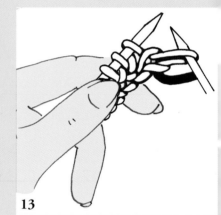

Fig. 10 – Put the needle with the cast on stitches in your left hand. Holding the yarn behind that needle, put the tip of the other needle into the first stitch at the end of the left needle, behind the needle with the cast on stitches.

Fig. 11 – Holding both needles in your left hand, use your right index finger to push the yarn from the skein under and over the point of the right needle.

Fig. 12 – Pull the yarn through the stitch with the right needle.

Fig. 13 – Push that stitch from the left needle to the right needle. Repeat the process in Figures 10 through 13 until all your stitches are on the right needle. This makes one row. Switch hands and repeat the process until you have made the number of rows you need.

BINDING OFF

When you have made the number of rows you need, you must bind off to finish. Do not pull these stitches too tight – loose is best, so the piece doesn't get pulled out of shape.

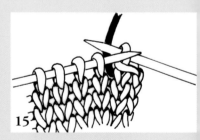

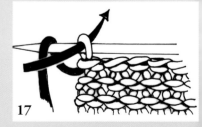

Fig. 14 – Knit the first two stitches on the left needle onto the right needle. Put the tip of the left needle into the first stitch you knit onto the right needle.

Fig. 15 – Move the stitch completely off the right needle. You now have one stitch on the right needle. The first stitch is bound off!

Fig. 16 – Knit another stitch. Lift the first stitch over the top of the second as before. Continue until there are no stitches remaining on the left needle.

Fig. 17 – Cut the yarn, leaving a 6" to 8" tail. Pull the tail through the last stitch to tie it off. Use a large-eye tapestry needle to weave the tail into the edge of the knitted piece.

How to Knit

THE PURL STITCH

The purl stitch is the reverse of the knit stitch. Instead of holding the yarn in back of the needles, you hold it in front.

Fig. 18 – Put the point of the right needle into the first stitch on the left needle, going from the back into the front of the stitch.

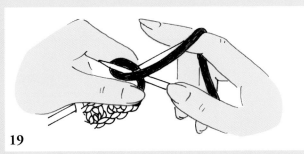

Fig. 19 – Bring the yarn around the right needle in a clockwise direction with your right index finger.

KNITTING IN FRONT & IN BACK OF THE SAME STITCH

Fig. 22 – Knit into the designated stitch on the left needle, but do not drop the stitch off the left needle.

Fig. 23 – Move the needle toward the back of the work, and knit into the back of the same stitch. Drop the old stitch off the left needle, creating two stitches from one stitch.

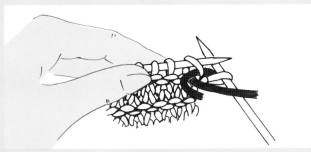

Fig. 20 – Ease the yarn backward through the stitch, using the point of the needle in your right hand.

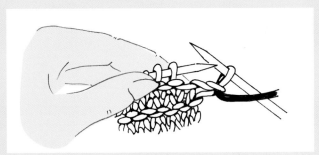

Fig. 21 – Slip the stitch off the left needle and onto the right needle. Repeat the process until all the stitches have been moved to the right needle.

Needle Felting Gallery

This section shows you more items created with needle felting, including pins and brooches, hats and head bands, a purse and a tote, a decorated sweater – even a landscape wall piece. Be inspired!

Garden Pin

by Nancy Hoerner

A needle felted background brings together the greens of the garden. Blanket stitching with pearl cotton accents the edges. The same thread is used to attach a twig. Contrasting color is provided by a floral polymer clay bead that sits atop needle felted dimensional leaves.

Birthday Candles Pin

by Judy McDowell

A wet-felted black rectangle is the background for colorful needle felted embellishments.

Book Brooch

by Nancy Hoerner

A felted rectangle has a slanted pocket that holds a tiny book of handmade paper with a string binding finished with beaded flowers. There's room for a small pencil or pen, as well.

Knitted Purse with Felted Embellishments

by Kay Kaduce

Needle felting and beads embellish a hand-knitted purse.

Fluted Fancy Hat

by Christy Skuban

A round-top felted hat is decorated with felted swirls of color. The wide brim is tacked in place to the sides of the crown.

Sparkling Squiggles Tote Bag

by Judy Jacobs

A two-tone tote bag was felted over a large bolster to achieve the shape. It provides the background for an all-over squiggly design of sparkling yarn with hits of bright color. The felted purple flowers combine petals and a trumpet shape with metallic yarn centers that are placed over pairs of deep green leaves.

Embellished Sweater

by Deb Zanoni

A simple white sweater is embellished with a needle felted collar and body appliques that extend down the back and on both sides of the front. Yarn tassels and edging and an assortment of beads add texture and shine.

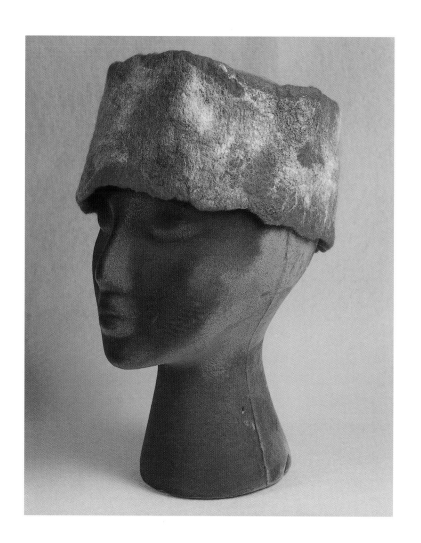

Head Bands

by Suzanne from Hookedonfelt.com

Two head bands from the same artist take differing approaches. The dramatic black-and-white band sports just a few dots of pink, a smooth and even bottom edge, and black feathers along the top edge. The deep pink band has uneven edges and a multitude of colors.

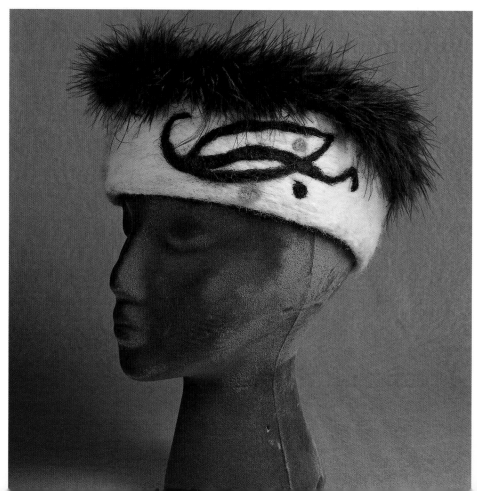

Felted Landscape

by Judy Hable

The trees, the rocks, the water, the sky – all are made of felted wool.
This picture is the Artist's view from her cabin on Madeline Island
in Lake Superior.

Metric Conversion Chart

Inches to Millimeters and Centimeters

Inches	MM	CM	Inches	MM	CM
1/8	3	.3	2	51	5.1
1/4	6	.6	3	76	7.6
3/8	10	1.0	4	102	10.2
1/2	13	1.3	5	127	12.7
5/8	16	1.6	6	152	15.2
3/4	19	1.9	7	178	17.8
7/8	22	2.2	8	203	20.3
1	25	2.5	9	229	22.9
1-1/4	32	3.2	10	254	25.4
1-1/2	38	3.8	11	279	27.9
1-3/4	44	4.4	12	305	30.5

Yards to Meters

Yards	Meters	Yards	Meters
1/8	.11	3	2.74
1/4	.23	4	3.66
3/8	.34	5	4.57
1/2	.46	6	5.49
5/8	.57	7	6.40
3/4	.69	8	7.32
7/8	.80	9	8.23
1	.91	10	9.14
2	1.83		

Index

A

Adhesive, fabric 20, 24, 26, 52, 72

Amulet Bag 90

Appendix 114

B

Bag 90

Beaded Fantasy Bracelet 96

Beads 20, 24, 58, 64, 66, 72, 76, 89, 91, 92, 93, 95, 98, 99

    felt bracelet 96

    felt necklace 99

    felt round 88, 89

    felt tube 87, 91, 92, 95,

    glass 26, 62, 91, 96

    seed 24, 52, 54, 56, 58, 72, 76, 96, 98, 112

Bird 98

Black Jacket with Felted Yoke 61

Blanket 46, 82

Bold Traveler with Beaded Flap 23

Bolster 26, 40

Bracelet 92, 94, 95, 96

Button(s) 32, 62, 72, 112

C

Cape 34

Cape of Cloud Jacket 72

Cardigan 68

Chain 90

Charm 90, 95

Clasp, jewelry 89, 91, 99

Closure 20, 24, 26, 32, 35

Cloud(s) see *Wool*

Clutch 30

Colorful Strands Cardigan 68

Counting Sheep Blanket Throw 82

Craft knife 43, 93

Crochet hook 20, 24, 26, 30, 72, 96

Crochet, how to 114

Cutting a Stencil 43

Cutting mat 43

D

Daisy 46

Denim 54, 56, 66

Diamond Felted Bracelet 92

Dog cape 34

Dragonfly Dimension Pillow 58

E

Electric burner 43

Embellished Bead Necklaces 99

F

Fabric 26, 92

Fabric, making 14

Face(s) 108

Fall Fantasy Flower 106

Fancy Flowered Denim Skirt 56

Fashion Circle Pendant Necklace 93

Felt, craft 90, 92

Felted Flower Tote 52

Felting

    Design with Stencils 42

    Glossary 9

    history 8

    needles 11

    the Design 44

Fibers 12

Fleece 46, 64

Flower(s) 41, 46, 52, 54, 56, 104, 105, 106

Flowers & Leaves 104

Foam 11, 20, 24, 30, 32, 35, 46, 48, 52, 54, 56, 58, 62, 64, 66, 68, 72, 76, 80, 82, 89, 90, 92, 93, 95, 96, 98, 99, 106, 108, 112

Foam Work Surface 11

Free Form Felting 60

G

Gallery 118

Glossary 9

Gussied Up Tote 30

H

Handles 20, 24, 30

Hat(s) 38, 112, 120

Head band(s) 124

Head pin 93

Heathered Fleece Jacket 64

Hills & Valleys Denim Jacket 66

How to Crochet a Chain 114

How to Knit 115, 117

I

Introduction 8

Iron 17, 20, 24, 26, 30, 32, 45, 46, 48, 52, 54, 56, 58, 62, 64, 66, 72, 80, 82, 90

J

Jacket 61, 62, 64, 66, 72, 76

Jeans 54

Jewelry 86

Josieåfs Cape 34

Jump ring 90

K

Knit, how to 115

Knitting needles, see *needles*

Continued on next page

Index

L

Leaves 104, 105

M

Making

Faces 108

Felt Fabric 14

Felt Jewelry 86

Felted Embellishments 102

Round Beads 88

Tube Beads 87

Marker 43

Masking tape 46, 48, 52, 54, 56

Memory wire 95

Memory Wire Bracelet 94

Modern Art Clutch 32

Multi-Strand Necklace 91

Mutli-needle tool 11, 20, 24, 26, 30, 32, 35, 40, 62, 64, 66, 68, 72, 76, 80, 91, 92, 95, 96, 106, 108

N

Nail polish 89, 91

Necklace(s) 89, 91, 90, 93, 99

Needle Felted Hats 38

Needle Felting Gallery 118

Needle Felting Supplies 10

Needle(s)

beading 20, 24, 52, 54, 56, 58, 62, 64, 66, 72, 76, 80, 91, 92, 96, 98, 112

felting 11, 20, 24, 26, 30, 32, 35, 40, 46, 48, 52, 54, 56, 58, 62, 64, 66, 68, 72, 80, 82, 89, 90, 91, 92, 93, 95, 96, 98, 99, 106, 108, 112

knitting 20, 30, 72

sewing 30, 32, 35, 68, 72, 76, 80, 92, 99, 106, 108

tapestry 20, 24, 26, 30, 35

P

Pattern 26, 27, 37, 46, 51, 78, 84, 107

Pencil 82

Pillow 58

cover 58

form 58

Pin 98, 106, 118

Pin back 98, 106

Pins

safety 48

straight 26, 30, 35, 96

Pliers

needlenose 20, 24, 26, 30, 32, 96

roundnose 93, 95

Pretty Petals Jacket 76

Purse 19, 24, 26, 119

R

Retro Sophisticate Purse 26

Roving, see *wool*

Ruffled Clutch Purse 19

Ruler 92

S

Safety Tips 13

Scissors 92

Sequins 54, 56, 58

Sewing machine 26

Silk & Sparkle Embellished Hat 112

Silk 112

Skirt 56

Snap 92

Snowflake 48

Stencil 44, 46, 48, 52, 54, 56, 58

blank 43

cutting 43

felting with 42

Supplies, needle felting 10

Sweater 48, 62, 68, 80, 121, 123

T

Thread

beading 20, 52, 54, 56, 58, 64, 66, 72, 89, 91, 92, 96, 98, 99, 112

decorative 64

sewing 20, 24, 26, 30, 32, 35, 62, 68, 72, 76, 80, 90, 106, 108

Tissue paper 82

Tote 28, 52, 121

Trim 26

Trimmed in Style Sweater 80

Tropical Bird Pin 98

V

Vine & Flower Jeans 54

W

Wall hanging 125

Warm & Comfy Fleece Throw 46

Winter Wardrobe Necklace 89

Winter's Here Snowflake Sweater 48

Wire 26, 96, 98

Wire cutters 26, 93, 95, 96

Wool

clouds 12, 15, 20, 24, 26, 30, 32, 35, 40, 44, 46, 48, 52, 54, 62, 64, 72, 90, 98, 99, 106, 108, 112

roving 12, 18, 20, 24, 30, 32. 35, 40, 44, 46, 48, 52, 54, 56, 58, 62, 66, 68, 76, 89, 91, 92, 93, 95, 96, 98, 99, 108

Y

Yarn 20, 24, 26, 30, 35, 40, 62, 68, 72, 76, 80, 82, 96, 98, 106, 108, 112